POWERPRO SERIES

How To Restore
AUTOMOTIVE ELECTRICS

MBI Publishing
Company

First published in 1996 by MBI Publishing Company, 729 Prospect Avenue, PO Box 1, Osceola, WI 54020-0001 USA

MBI Publishing Company books are also available at discounts in bulk quantity for industrial or sales-promotional use. For details write to Special Sales Manager at Motorbooks International Wholesalers & Distributors, 729 Prospect Avenue, PO Box 1, Osceola, WI 54020-0001 USA.

Library of Congress Cataloging-in-Publication Data

Aird, Forbes.
    How to restore automotive electrics/Forbes Aird.
        p. cm.
    Includes bibliographical references and index.
        ISBN 0-7603-0120-4 (alk. paper)
    1. Automobiles—Electric equipment—Maintenance and repair. 2. Automobiles—Conservation and restoration. I. Title.
TL272.A25   1996
629.25'4'0288—dc20   96-8846

On the front cover: This collage was assembled from parts supplied by Little Dearborn in Minneapolis, Minnesota, and parts and test equipment from the shop of Neil Yerigan. *Randy Johnson*

On the back cover: Left: A dual-voltage battery can be an elegant solution to the problem of retaining a car's originality as well as the best performance. Right: A cutaway illustration of a 1939 Ford flathead starter motor. *Courtesy Ford Canada.*

Printed in the United States of America

Contents

Acknowledgments

Several people contributed significantly to making this book possible. I wish to express my sincere appreciation, first and foremost, to Gord Green, who patiently answered endless questions, offered support and encouragement, and reviewed the final text. Thanks are also due to Green's boss, Bob deBruyn, of Detronics in Stouffville, Ontario, for tolerating with good humor the demands I made on the time of his most valuable employee.

Ross Reinhart of Antique Auto Electric, Goderich, Ontario, also generously gave of his time and provided most of the rare parts that appear in the illustrations. I am indebted to John Arnone and Sandy Notarianni for allowing me access to the historical files of Ford of Canada, and for trusting me with archival photos and publications. Thanks also to Stu Low and Frank Agueci of General Motors (GM) Canada for providing further illustrations.

For other illustrations and information I am indebted to Gene and Donna at YnZ's Yesterday's Parts; the Lanes at Antique Auto Battery Manufacturing Co.; Harnesses Unlimited; Optima Batteries, Inc.; Bathurst, Inc.; John Eagles; Jamie Mullins and Klein Tools/VACO; and to Brian Foster, Steve Hire, and Janna Drinkard of Cooper Tools/Weller.

Introduction

It should come as no surprise that levers and gears and pushrods and cams and screw threads came hundreds or even thousands of years before solenoids and condensers and generators and light bulbs.

People come to understand their world first by sight and touch and taste and sound. And while a case can be made that smell and taste leave the deepest impression, touch and sight probably connect best with conscious awareness. So it makes sense that when humankind started making things, rather than just using what they found lying on the ground, those early tools and objects were purely mechanical—clubs and axes and levers and wedges. (The only essential difference between a wedge and a screw thread, or between a lever and a gear, is that the motion goes around in circles.)

Likewise, if you can watch something work, you can generally figure out how it operates. Even if it's broken, you can trace how this pushes on that, how the "thingumajig" turns the "watchemacallit," and... hey! This little pin here has fallen out!

Electricity, though, is invisible. It's hard to come to grips with because we can't see it, can't directly touch it, can't hear or smell it. So, while many auto enthusiasts will happily wade into a piece of machinery they've never encountered before, when faced with anything to do with electricity, their confidence sinks. They suddenly remember that they have to mow the lawn, that there's an important phone call they have to make, that the Raiders are playing the Bears on Channel 7. Electrical stuff is for experts—the guys that can make a radar detector out of an old Stromberg Carlson radio, a couple of war-surplus field telephone's and a bunch of wire.

Well, maybe so, if you're talking about a cavity magnetron, or an integrated circuit chip, or a laser—but not when it comes to the electrical parts of automobiles built before, say, 1960. If you exclude the stuff that it would be impractical to work on, for financial reasons, even if you had a Ph.D. in electrical engineering and decades of experience, because the cost of the necessary tools and test equipment exceeds the cost of a new unit or a pro's time, then there is an encouraging truth to bear in mind: Every electrical fault in these older vehicles is, at some level, a mechanical fault. *Electricity never fails!* It's always a matter of something broken or missing or burned or covered with crud. Always.

True, a wire that is broken inside its insulation can't immediately be seen, and neither can a burned contact in a voltage regulator, nor the layer of corrosion between a battery post and the cable terminal. But it's *capable* of being seen. And, once you know how to test for it, it's capable of being found and fixed. While electricity can never fail, mechanical stuff can, so electrical *systems* can fail as a result. That's why so much of the electrical apparatus on new cars is made up of purely electronic components such as transistors and integrated circuits, rather than mechanical switches and electromechanical relays—there's less hardware to break down, which is a major reason why modern cars are so much more reliable than those of 40 or 50 years ago, and why they need so much less maintenance.

In these pages we'll attempt, for the purist, to show how to get the most out of an original system—or at least one that *looks* original. For the restorer who puts reliable operation ahead of authentic appearance, we'll suggest some ways to upgrade an old electrical system, including changing from 6 volts to 12. For all readers, we hope to dispel some of the mystery surrounding automotive electrics, how to find faults in the systems used in older cars, and how to fix them. Of course, we cannot hope to detail every piece of electrical apparatus used on every model of every car, so a book of this type is no substitute for the shop manual for your particular vehicle. Used in conjunction with that specific information, however, it should help you rehabilitate the electrics on your older car to the same standards you would set for a mechanical restoration.

You may be tempted to skip past the first chapter, which deals with general electrical and magnetic principles. We urge you not to. While much of this work can be done on a "'monkey-see-monkey-do" basis, there is no manual so detailed that you won't run into situations that aren't covered. When that happens, the only way to proceed is to think the problem through. The basic material in chapter one will help you keep your thinking straight. Above all, remember, there is no magic; you too can be an expert.

Basic Electricity and Magnetism

1

A reasonable place to start a book like this would be to explain what electricity is. Well, sorry to disappoint you, but we can't do that. Nobody can. For all that has been learned over the centuries about electricity, nobody really knows what it is. Not to worry, though; one thing we have learned is that, as with other basic forces in the universe that can't be "explained" in any real way (like gravity, for instance), electricity operates according to a fixed set of rules. Once we know what those rules are, we can make it work for us, as reliably as the sunrise, without needing to understand it in a fundamental way. We can build various sorts of instruments and machinery that use electricity to perform useful tasks, we can confidently predict what electrical apparatus and circuits will do under different conditions, and we can fix 'em when they're broken. And even though we can't explain electricity, we can go some way toward describing how it works.

Two Kinds of "Juice"

To get a handle on a mysterious subject, one way to proceed is by analogy: We can construct in our minds a model that parallels the thing we don't understand, but that works in a way we *do* understand. The usual analogy, or model, for electricity is water.

If we drill a hole in the bottom of a tank full of water, then

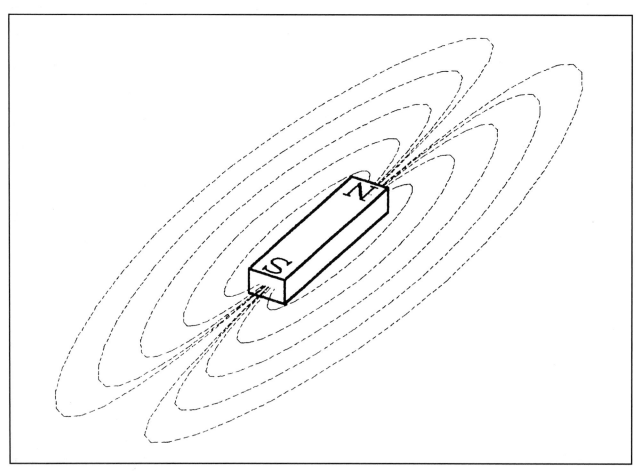

A field of magnetic force lines surrounds every magnet. Though invisible, it can be seen if iron filings are sprinkled on a piece of paper held above the magnet.

put a finger over the hole to plug it, we will be able to feel the pressure of the water pushing against our finger. How great that pressure is depends on just one thing—the height of the water level in the tank. This pressure is the analogy for voltage.

If we then remove our finger, the water will flow out of the tank at a certain rate (expressed in gallons per minute [gpm]), according to the pressure behind it, and the size of the hole; obviously, a small hole will restrict the flow more than a large one. The rate of flow is an analogy for the electrical concept of current. The size of the hole is an analogy for electrical resistance.

Units of Measurement
To get beyond such general statements—to be able to quantify our predictions, in other words—we need some units of measurement. Water pressure is measured in pounds per square inch (psi); the electrical equivalent is volts. Similarly, we measure flow in gpm; the unit of electrical flow is the ampere, often abbreviated to "amp." Likewise, we can talk about the restriction to water flow in terms of the hole diameter in inches. (Actually, we should use "one divided by the hole diameter," because a big hole restricts less than a small one; otherwise a big number would mean a small restriction.) The unit of electrical resistance is the ohm, often represented by the symbol "Ω." Here, the numbers work the right way around—more ohms means more resistance. The following list shows the relationship between the analogous units for water and electricity:

Water	Electricity
Pressure (psi)	Voltage (volts)
Flow (gpm)	Current (amps)
Restriction (1/hole diameter)	Resistance (ohms)

There's another unit of measurement we need to know about—the watt, which is a measure of electrical power. If we direct the flow of water from our imaginary tank over a paddle wheel, the wheel will tend to turn, and we could use that turning wheel to do useful work—to grind corn, say. The rate at which we could grind corn would depend on the power we extract from the wheel (expressed in horsepower), which, in turn, is determined both by the rate of flow through the wheel and by the pressure behind it. By the same analogy, the power we can get from a flow of electricity depends on both the voltage and the current. The formulas for calculating power for each follow:

Electricity operates according to a fixed set of rules. Once we know what those rules are, we can make it work for us,

---

water power (hp) = pressure (psi) x flow (gpm)

electrical power (watts) = pressure (volts) x flow (amps)

These are just two of several different ways of denoting power, but since power is power, no matter what the source, the units can be converted from one to the other. In this case, 746 watts equals one horsepower.

DC Circuits
Beyond this point, we must admit, our "electricity = water" analogy starts to fall apart. While water will flow out of a tank with a hole in the bottom, or out of a pipe hooked up to that tank, electricity will not flow out of, say, a battery sitting by itself on the floor, or out of the exposed end of a wire hooked up to that battery. To do anything useful with electricity, we need a circuit—a continuous loop. We could stretch our analogy a bit and consider the example of a water pipe with its two ends connected together. If we put a pump someplace in the loop to push the water around the circuit, then we could put a paddle wheel someplace else in the loop and so get some useful work out of the circuit. If you cut the pipe, though, the water would run out onto the ground, and the pump would have nothing to push, so to get any useful work from the paddle wheel you have to return the water to the suction side of the pump. To avoid making things more complicated than they need to be, however, let's just take it on faith that we have to start thinking in terms of circuits.

How does electricity flow through (or, more correctly, *around*) a circuit? First, consider that everything in the universe is made up of atoms, and atoms themselves are made up of smaller particles called electrons and protons. A proton has a small positive electrical charge; an electron has a small negative electrical charge. Usually, there is an equal number of electrons and protons in an atom, so the two charges cancel each other out, and the atom as a whole is electrically neutral. In certain kinds of atoms, like the ones that make up most metals, some of the electrons are comparatively loosely connected and can fairly easily be persuaded to separate themselves from one atom and to attach themselves to another adjacent atom.

If, for example, we arrange to stuff an extra electron into the end of a piece of copper, the electron will latch on to the closest atom, forcing another electron loose from that atom. That "free" electron will then nudge an electron out of the next adjacent atom, which, in turn, will shove yet another electron loose from the next atom, and so on down the line, like a row of dominoes, until one electron pops out of the other end of the piece of copper. Remember, though, that the electron we stuff in has to come from someplace, and the electron that pops out has to go to someplace; we have to keep thinking in terms of a circuit.

Materials that behave like the piece of copper in the above scenario are called conductors. Copper is an excellent conductor of electricity; silver is even better. Aluminum isn't quite as ready as copper or silver to have its electrons swap places, but it is still a pretty good conductor; iron is somewhat less so. Materials like wood and fiberglass and rubber, on the other hand, hang on to their electrons with such a firm grip that, for all practical purposes, you can't make an electric current flow through them. Such materials are called insulators. In between the two is a category of conductor called a resistor—something that offers a significant amount of flow restriction, without completely obstructing it.

Even though conductors allow electrons to flow through them with little opposition, they still fight back to a certain extent, so they possess a certain amount of resistance. Now, we know that the pressure drop between two points in a pipe carrying a flow of water depends on the smoothness or roughness of the interior of the pipe; likewise, the amount of resistance a conductor offers depends on what kind of material it is made from. Good conductors, like copper, can be thought of as smooth pipes. Water flow also depends on the cross section area of the pipe—it is easier to get water to flow through a big pipe than a small one. Equally, fat copper wires create less electrical resistance than skinny ones. Again, just as water flow dwindles to a trickle when you hook up several garden hoses end-to-end, the resistance of a conductor also increases with its length. That is, long wires create more resistance than short ones. All conductors, then, are resistors to a small degree. (In practice, the distinction between a resistor and a conductor is whether we are deliberately trying to restrict current flow, or whether we are trying to reduce that restriction to the barest minimum.)

If you measure the pressure at any two points between

To do anything useful with electricity, we need a circuit—a continuous loop.

---

the beginning and the end of pipes of various diameters and lengths carrying a flow of water, you'll find that the pressure difference between those two points inevitably increases as you progress along the pipe and that there is a sharp drop anyplace there is a sudden restriction in the pipe. Similarly, when a current flows around an electrical circuit, there will be a voltage drop between any two points, and the size of the voltage drop will depend on the resistance the current encounters between those two points.

Even if there are no actual resistors in the circuit (apart from the small amount of resistance accounted for by the conductors themselves), everything that uses the juice to do something useful—a light bulb, a motor, a heater—can only do its job by converting some of the electrical energy into another form. Now, if we measured the pressure near the corn-grinding paddle wheel in our water-pipe model, we would discover a pressure difference between the inlet and the outlet sides, because as it turns the current of water into work, the paddle wheel necessarily impedes the flow. In the same way, there will be a voltage drop across each component in an electrical circuit that is converting the electrical energy into some other form. From the electrical point of view, then, each component is a load.

Just as the size of the pressure drop across the paddle wheel would depend on how much power we were taking out of it at the time—how hard we are loading it—so the size of the voltage drop across an electrical component will depend on how much resistance the component has, which in turn is a measure of how much of something else—light, shaft power, heat—it is "making" out of the electricity. (Incidentally, this works both ways. To create a resistance, we have to "make" something; we have to convert the electrical energy into something else. A resistor, for instance, "makes" heat.) Equally, everything we do that introduces a restriction into a circuit, whether electrical or hydraulic, will also diminish the rate of flow around the loop. These relationships between current, voltage, and resistance are neatly summarized by Ohm's Law.

Ohm's Law
While workers in other areas of electricity and electronics have to learn and remember a whole bag-full of formulas and equations, the electrical systems of automobiles before the early 1970s are sufficiently simple that (thankfully!) we can figure out just about everything we need to know using just a few very simple rules. Ohm's Law is one of these and the most basic one.

We've mentioned the obvious connections between the water pressure at the bottom of our imaginary tank, the size of the hole, and the rate of water flow. If we know any two of these factors, we can figure out the third. Likewise, Ohm's Law allows us to figure voltage or current or resistance if we know what the values for the other two are. In truth, the calculation for water flow is actually more complicated, because the restriction caused by the hole does not vary directly with its diameter—to predict the flow we would need to calculate the *area* of the hole, and then make some additional correction for its shape. Electricity is simpler!

Ohm's Law is as follows:

current (amps) = voltage (volts)/resistance (ohms)

So, if we know that the resistance to flow is 1 ohm, and the "pressure" is 1 volt, then 1 amp will flow. Crank up the voltage to 6 volts, and 6 amps will flow. Keep the voltage at 6 and double the resistance to 2 ohms, and then the current will be 3 amps. Simple enough?

We can turn Ohm's Law around to calculate voltage, if we know the current and resistance in the circuit:

voltage (volts) = current (amps) x resistance (ohms)

So, if we know that the current is, say, 3 amps, and the resistance is 4 ohms, then we must be dealing with a "pressure" of 12 volts. Keep the resistance the same, but change the current to 1 amp, then the voltage must equal 3.

Finally, we can turn around Ohm's Law yet again to calculate resistance if the voltage and current are known:

resistance (ohms) = voltage (volts)/current (amps)

If we know that we have 9 volts of "pressure" and we measure a current of 1/10 of an ampere, then the resistance must be 90 ohms.

Series and Parallel Circuits

It's important to realize that in a simple, single loop or circuit the rate of flow is the same no matter where in the circuit you measure it, and no matter what resistance exists between one point and another. This may seem puzzling at first, but think in terms of a water pipe again. All the water that goes in the pipe has to come out, and it has to be coming out at the same rate it's going in—you can't make a gallon of water disappear, even temporarily. While some simple electrical circuits are, in fact, just a single loop, there is another possibility.

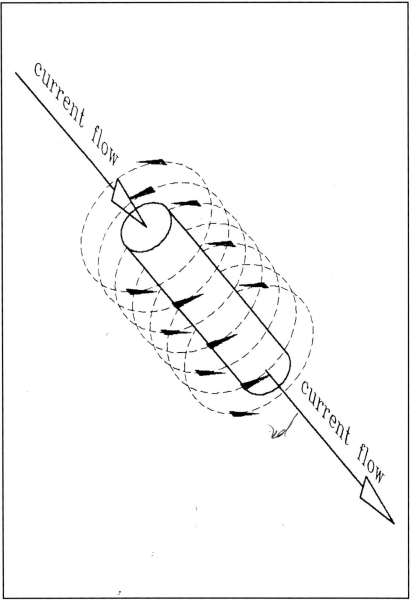

When a conductor is carrying an electric current, it exhibits a magnetic field, just like a permanent magnet.

Continuing with our water model, note that two garden hoses can be hooked together in two different ways. You can couple them end to end, or you can screw a "Y" adapter onto your outdoor faucet, connect one hose to each branch of the "Y," and then couple the two hoses together again with another "Y" connector at the other end. In the first case, the hoses are connected in series; in the second case, they are in parallel. Now, if you turned the faucet on all the way and measured how long it took to fill a bucket, using both hoses, you would discover that the parallel connection worked better than the series connection. What's more, it would fill the bucket faster than one hose alone, directly connected to the faucet.

Also, if you measured the difference in pressure between the faucet and the outlet at the bucket, you would discover that the pressure drop is least with the parallel setup and greatest with the series connection. The single hose would fall somewhere in between. You can actually check this out, if you don't believe us. If you did, you would have gotten two things—wet feet, and a good start on understanding the next couple of laws it is helpful to know if you're going to mess around with an automobile electrical system.

Resistance Laws
The total resistance of a series is simply the sum of the separate resistances. Thus, a 100-ohm resistance connected to the end of a 200-ohm resistance yields a total resistance of 300 ohms. Add a 50-ohm resistor to the end of that and the total becomes 350 ohms. Dead simple.

In series:

$$R(total) = R1 + R2 + R3 . .$$

So, the resistance of a 50-ohm resistor connected in series with a 100-ohm resistor and a 250-ohm resistor would be 400 ohms, as shown below:

$$R(total) = 50 \text{ ohms} + 100 \text{ ohm} + 250 \text{ ohms}$$

$$R(total) = 400 \text{ ohms}$$

When resistors act in parallel, though, the juice can take more than one route, which reduces the obstruction to a value below that of any one resistor considered separately, just like the two hoses hooked to a "Y." The general rule for calculating resistance in parallel is as follows:

$$1/R(total) = 1/R1 + 1/R2 + 1/R3 . . .$$

The rate of flow is the same no matter where in the circuit you measure it, and no matter what resistance exists between one point and another.

So, the resistance of a 100-ohm resistor connected in parallel with one of 200 ohms is calculated as follows:

$$1/R(total) = 1/100 \text{ ohms} + 1/200 \text{ ohms}$$

First, convert to similar units, making 1/100 ohms 2/200 ohms

$$1/R(total) = 2/200 \text{ ohms} + 1/200 \text{ ohms}$$

Invert the result to obtain the correct resistance:

$$R(total) = 200 \text{ ohms}/3$$

$$R(total) = 66.7 \text{ ohms}$$

And if we add the extra 50-ohm resistor in parallel with the other two, the resistance can be calculated as follows:

$$1/R(total) = 1/100 \text{ ohms} + 1/200 \text{ ohms} + 1/50 \text{ ohms}$$

$$1/R(total) = 2/200 \text{ ohms} + 1/200 \text{ ohms} + 4/200 \text{ ohms}$$

$$1/R(total) = 7/200 \text{ ohms}$$

$$R(total) = 200/7 \text{ ohms}$$
$$R(total) = 28.6 \text{ ohms}$$

When there are just two resistors, this general form can be simplified a bit, as follows:

$$R(total) = (R1 \times R2)/ (R1 + R2)$$

Shorts and Open Circuits
What happens if we construct a circuit with no load—no resistance? If you connected the positive (+) terminal of a battery directly to the negative (-) with a jumper cable, you would create such a circuit. It's called a short circuit (or "short" for, uh, short), and with good reason—it couldn't get any shorter, could it? Now, in truth, there is *some* resistance in this circuit—the jumper cable will have some slight resistance, and the battery has some internal resistance. (This last doesn't usually figure in any of our calculations about what is going on elsewhere in an automotive circuit, though.) Still, the overall resistance in this case is about as low as possible, so current will flow at an enormous rate through this circuit. Zillions of electrons will whistle out of the battery terminal that has an excess of them, through the jumper, and into the terminal that has an electron deficit, where they make violent chemistry, causing the battery to fume and bubble. Not to mention the fact that the jumper cable will get red hot from the colossal amperage.

Any connection that joins the "hot lead" (the pressure side of the pump, if you like) to "ground" (the suction side), without its passing through a load, creates such a short circuit. The results are twofold: first, whatever device is supposed to be getting the power won't work; second, the huge current will act on the slight resistance of the conductor to create a lot of heat. Shorts are a serious problem that can create a fire hazard. To protect against them, we use fuses, circuit breakers, and fusible links.

An open circuit, on the other hand, allows no current to flow at all. In fact, an open circuit isn't really a circuit—anyplace the circuit is open, the continuous loop is broken. Switches create open circuits when they are turned off; so do broken wires or connectors; and if enough corrosion or paint or other insulator is present in a circuit, that too will effectively break the loop and produce an "open."

Voltage Drops in a Series Circuit

We noted above that the rate of current flow in a circuit with components connected in series (that is, forming a single loop) is the same no matter where you measure it, no matter what the resistance between one point and another. What varies is the voltage. A final useful rule to remember, then: The voltage drops around a series circuit always add up to zero.

At first glance, this makes no sense at all. In a simple circuit consisting of just a 12-volt battery and a light bulb, there are 12 volts across the battery (a difference of 12 volts between the two terminals), and 12 volts across the bulb—that makes 24 volts, not zero. To make sense out of this, you have to pay attention to the "pluses" and the "minuses"—the difference between a "hot" and a "ground" terminal, if you like.

Pluses, Minuses, and Grounds

The conventional way of describing current flow is *from* a positive *to* a negative. Recall, though, that an electrical current is a flow of electrons, and electrons are negatively charged particles, so paradoxically and confusingly, they flow *from* a "negative" terminal—one where there is a surplus of electrons—*to* a "positive" terminal—one where there is a shortage of electrons, or an excess of protons, which is the same thing. To avoid hopeless confusion, we'll stick with the conventional way of describing current flow—*from* positive *to* negative.

Now, in an automobile electrical system, one terminal of the battery is connected to something called ground. Just what the heck is ground? All the term "ground" really means is that we have chosen some arbitrary place in the circuit to start measuring from. By convention, that place is the connection to the ground terminal of the battery. In all current automobiles, that terminal is the one marked "-" (but many early cars were positive ground). Never forget that we have to keep thinking in terms of a circuit—a complete loop—and, in automobiles, the ground is the other half of every circuit. It's not actually invisible, as some would say, but it *is* in disguise—the conductor that forms one half of most circuits is the steel in the vehicle's chassis.

In a negative ground system, then, the positive terminal at the battery will show +12 volts compared to ground. From ground to the hot lead is +12 volts. But at the bulb, the 12 volts is from the hot lead to ground; measuring in the same direction as we measured the battery (that is, from ground to the hot lead) we would see -12 volts. Plus 12 and minus 12 adds up to zero.

To demonstrate this rule, known as von Kirschoff's Law, and to gain a bit of practice with

Ohm's Law, let's consider a circuit consisting of a 12-volt battery and two different light bulbs, wired together in series. Let's say we measure the resistance of one bulb as being 3 ohms, and the other one shows 5 ohms. The total resistance, then, is 8 ohms.

From Ohm's Law:

current (amps) = voltage (volts)/resistance (ohms)

So the current flowing through the circuit is calculated as follows:

current (amps) = 12 volts/ 8 ohms

current (amps) = 1.5 amps

We've said that the current in a series circuit is the same everywhere (you can't make elec-

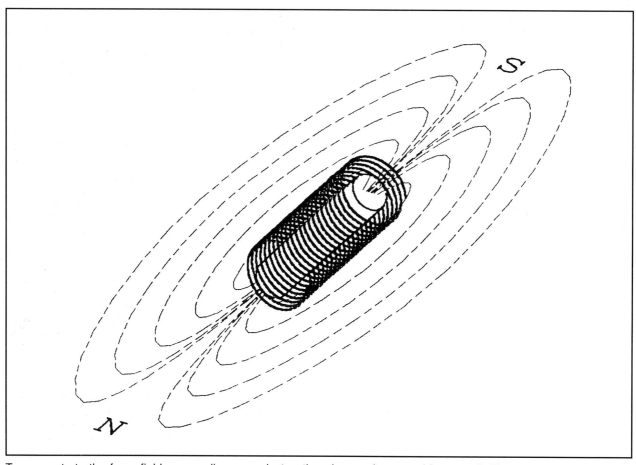

To concentrate the force field surrounding a conductor, the wire can be wound into a coil. The coil then becomes an electromagnet.

trons disappear any more than you can make water disappear), so each bulb must have 1.5 amps flowing through it. We can now figure out the voltage drop across each bulb separately, also using Ohm's Law.

For the first bulb:

voltage drop = 1.5 amps x 3 ohm

voltage drop = 4.5 volts
And for the second bulb:

voltage drop = 1.5 amps x 5 ohms

voltage drop = 7.5 volts

To calculate the total voltage drop across both bulbs, add the two voltage drops. Thus:

total voltage drop = 4.5 volts + 7.5 volts

total voltage drop = 12 volts

If you keep the pluses and minuses straight, this figure exactly cancels the 12 volts across the battery. Von Kirschoff was right! This means that you never have to calculate the last voltage drop in a series—it's always the value that will make the total around the circuit equal zero.

Magnetism
Electricity defies explanation, but at least we can grapple with it by talking about water in pipes. Magnetism, though, is worse. Not only can we not explain it, we can't even really describe it! Nev-

er mind; as before, we'll just plug along, counting on the fact that it always does the same thing under the same circumstances, so we can make it work for us.

A state can be produced in iron, nickel, alloys of the two, and a very few other materials, in which they exhibit the ability to apparently attract or repel each other. When in this state, a piece of one of these materials is called a magnet. This condition of magnetism allows a chunk of one of these materials to pick up an iron nail. What's more, the iron nail will then exhibit magnetism, too, so it can attract another piece of iron. If we magnetize two iron nails in this way, we will find that the nails either attract or repel each other, according to which ends are held near each other:

One end of each nail will attract one end of the other nail, but repel the other end, and vice versa.

As it turns out, the entire earth, too, is a magnet, and the pull of the earth's magnetism on a magnetized needle that is free to swivel will cause one end of the needle to point toward north, a discovery that had important consequences for navigation. For convenience, the opposite ends of a magnet are labeled "north" and "south." Not surprisingly the north end of the earth's magnet is at the North Pole—actually the *magnetic* North Pole, which isn't quite the same thing as true north, but it's close enough to be useful for navigation.

The fact that some invisible property of the earth can cause a compass needle to line up in a certain relative direction suggests that magnetism exists as a force field around the magnetized object. The existence of that force field—itself invisible—can be seen from the behavior of a compass needle or, in the case of smaller magnets, by sprinkling iron filings onto a piece of paper held close to the magnet. Each filing will take on a north and a south pole, and together, they will line up along the magnetic lines of force.

Relationship Between Magnetism and Electricity

Though neither we nor physicists can "explain" either electricity or magnetism, it is clear that there is some connection between the two. For instance, when an electrical current passes along a conductor, a compass needle held near the conductor will swing toward it or away, just as it would if we held it near a magnet. A flow of current, then, must induce a magnetic field in a conductor, turning it into an electromagnet. What's more, this phenomenon also works the other way around: When a conductor passes through a magnetic field, an electrical current will flow in the conductor. This strange effect is the basis of a great many electrical apparatus, including solenoids, motors, and generators.

For example, suppose we wind a length of copper wire into a coil (to concentrate the fields of force) and then pass a current through it. If we then stick an iron nail or other easily magnetized piece of metal into the middle of the coil, that core, as it is called, will exert a pull on any piece of iron held near it, just like an ordinary permanent magnet. This is the principle behind solenoids and relays. Even more useful, if we form a conductor carrying an electrical current into a loop and then place that loop so it crosses the lines of force of a magnet, the loop will swivel toward or away from the poles of the magnet, according to which pole is which, and which way the current is flowing. If we mount the loop so that the swiveling motion acts in a circle around a center, we have the beginnings of an electric motor.

Likewise, if we actively swivel the loop through the magnetic field, we can generate a flow of current in the loop. That, as you may have guessed, is the principle behind a generator or alternator. We'll pick up on these topics in the next chapter.

The Battery

Since the battery is usually considered to be the division point—the start and end—of each electrical circuit in a car, that is as good a place as any to start a survey of automotive electrical components.

If you take any two different metals, immerse them in a liquid electrolyte (usually an acid), and join them together electrically, a current of electricity will flow through the conductor that connects them. Eventually, one of the two metals will completely corrode away, and the acid will become weaker, ultimately turning into water, but in the meantime we have a battery. A battery, then, is a means for converting chemical energy into electrical energy—in a sense it is a way to store electricity, and for that reason it is often called a storage battery.

In an automobile, the battery provides the energy needed to operate the starting motor and the ignition system, to get the engine going from a standstill. Once the engine is running, the electricity taken out of the battery during start-up is replaced by an engine-driven generator of some sort (see chapter three). The battery may also supplement the generator from time to time, when the total demand for electricity exceeds the output of the generator. Another function of the battery is to help smooth out variations in the generator's output.

Battery Rating Scales

The traditional method of expressing the quantity of electricity a battery can deliver is in terms of amp-hours. One amp-hour is one amp of current flowing for one hour. For complex reasons, the number of amp-hours a battery can supply depends on the *rate* of discharge—more of the juice a battery "contains" becomes available if the instantaneous load is small. To take account of this effect, the amp-hour rating of a battery is always specified over a certain length of time. One 6-volt automotive battery, for example, is rated at 120 amp-hours at a 20-hour rate. In

---

> The amp-hour rating of a battery gives a useful measure of its ability to sustain a light load over a long period, but even then we have to bear in mind that the battery's voltage will constantly dwindle as it is gradually discharged.

---

other words, if the load was adjusted so that the battery was discharged continuously for 20 hours, an average current of 6 amps could be drawn all throughout that time, without its voltage dropping below some reference value. The same battery, though, has a rating of 152 amps at the 20-minute rate—the sizable current of 152 amps can be drawn without the voltage dropping below the reference value, *but*

only for one third of an hour. The short-term rate, then, is just

152 amps x 1/3 hour = 50.7 amp-hours

The amp-hour rating of a battery gives a useful measure of its ability to sustain a light load over a long period, such as leaving the vehicle parked with its side lights on or limping home after a generator failure, but even then we have to bear in mind that the battery's *voltage* will constantly dwindle as it is gradually discharged. More significantly, though, the sensitivity of a battery to its rate of discharge means that there is very little sensible connection between a battery's capacity in amp-hours and its suitability for starting an automobile engine, where what is called for is a very high current over a very brief time.

For that reason, while the older amp-hour method of rating is still used for applications such as golf carts and emergency exit lighting installations in buildings, where the rating has some meaning related to the intended use, a new method of rating was introduced a few years ago that describes battery performance in terms of cold cranking amps and reserve capacity.

Cold cranking amps, or CCA, is a measure of a battery's ability to deliver large currents for a brief time at low temperatures. The number is established by cooling the battery's electrolyte to 0 degrees F., then drawing as much current as the battery will tolerate without its voltage falling below 7.2 volts (for a nominal 12-volt battery; 3.6 volts for a nominal 6-volt battery). The value of the current drawn is then the CCA rating of the battery, which obviously gives a much better picture of the ability of the battery to start a cold engine than any amp-hour rate measured over hours or even minutes.

Reserve capacity, or RC, attempts to measure the battery's ability to support a small load over a longer time. In this case, the rating is a measure of the number of minutes the battery can deliver 25 amps without its voltage dropping below 10.5 volts, for a nominal 12-volt unit, or half that for a 6-volt one.

Battery Construction and Performance

An automotive storage battery uses sulfuric acid for the electrolyte and two forms of lead for the electrodes—the metal parts. The electrodes are formed as thin flat plates and are held

---

Cold cranking amps, or CCA, is a measure of a battery's ability to deliver large currents for a brief time at low temperatures.

---

apart by separators—insulating plates set between the electrodes that permit the plates to be packed closely together without actually touching. The separators are perforated to allow the electrolyte to surround the plates. The negative plates are made from plain metallic lead, while the positive plates are made from lead oxide, sometimes called sponge lead.

The plates are grouped together into cells, consisting of vertically arranged stacks of alternating positive and negative plates; the individual cells, each capable of producing a little more than 2 volts, are connected together in series. Three cells, then, make a 6-volt battery; 6 cells make a 12-volt battery. More or larger plates will increase the total amount of electricity the battery can store but, oddly, the voltage will remain the same.

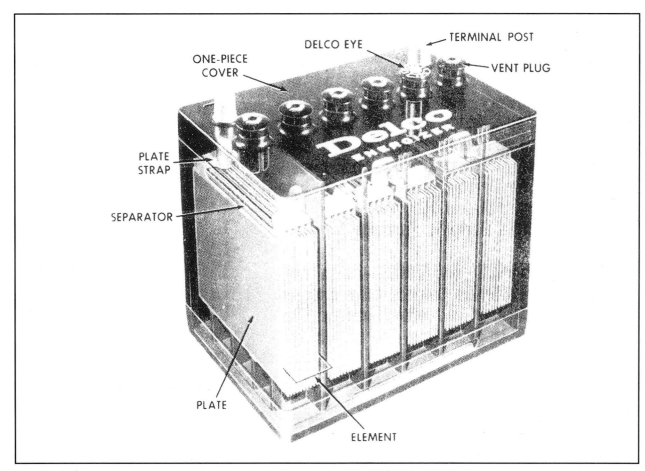

The alternating plates of lead and lead oxide, kept apart by separators, that form individual cells are visible in this "ghost" battery. This 12-volt unit has six cells; a 6-volt battery has just three. *Courtesy GM Canada*

To provide the necessary electrical connections, all the negative plates are connected together by a strap, and all the positive plates are connected by another strap. On older batteries, the straps are visible on top of the battery; in newer ones, these conductors are hidden beneath the top cover of the case. At either end of the battery, the end of the last strap is formed into a terminal. For years these terminals were tapered posts sticking up vertically; more modern designs place the terminals on the side of the case.

When we discharge a battery—when we draw current from it—the chemical process that produces electricity depletes both the electrodes and the electrolyte. If the battery is built with the right pair of metals, though, the process can be reversed by charging—forcing electricity back into the battery in the opposite direction. The metals will return to their original state, and the concentration of the acid will increase back to its original strength. Measuring the concen-

---

A fully charged lead-acid battery will show a specific gravity of about 1.26 to 1.27; a completely discharged one will measure as low as 1.10.

---

tration of the acid, then, gives us a useful gauge of the state of charge of the battery—how much juice is left in it.

The simplest way to measure this is with an instrument called a hydrometer—a device that looks like a turkey baster with a tiny float inside. When a small amount of electrolyte is drawn into the hydrometer by squeezing the bulb, the float will come to rest with more or less of itself sticking up above the fluid level, according to the specific gravity of the electrolyte—how much a fixed amount of it weighs in relation to water. Markings on the float allow a direct reading of the specific gravity. A fully charged lead-acid battery will show a specific gravity of about 1.26 to 1.27; a completely dis-

FLAME ARRESTER VENT CAPS

On older batteries, the straps that join the individual cells together are exposed above the top of the case. *Courtesy GM Canada*

charged one will measure as low as 1.10. (The specific gravity of pure water is 1.0.)

Although the conversion of chemical energy to electrical energy in a lead-acid battery can, in theory, be reversed indefinitely, there are several things that limit the life of a battery. For one thing, heat is created during the charging process, and that tends to boil off some of the water content in the electrolyte. The resulting increase in the concentration of the sulfuric acid can corrode the plates, reducing their effectiveness. Charging too rapidly or overcharging—trying to stuff more electricity into a battery that is "full"—will result in a rapid loss of electrolyte from this cause. In the case of severe overcharging the plates can become too hot, causing them to buckle so much that they touch and cause a short circuit.

Further, if the boiled-off water is replaced with ordinary tap water containing dissolved minerals and other impurities, the impurities will settle to the bottom of the case. Even though the plates are suspended a small distance above the bottom of the case, if enough of this sediment collects, it will form an electrical bridge across the plates, again causing them to short out.

For another thing, during discharge the chemistry between the plates and the sulfuric-acid electrolyte causes some of each plate to be converted from lead or sponge lead into lead sulfate. If a battery is left in a discharged state for a long time, the sulfate

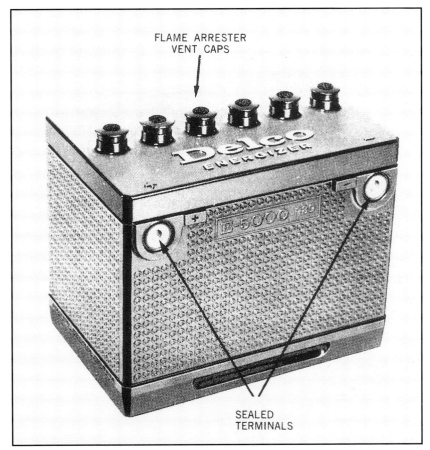

FLAME ARRESTER
VENT CAPS

SEALED
TERMINALS

In newer batteries the straps are concealed within the case. For a lower under-hood profile, modern batteries place the terminals on the side, rather than the top of the case. *Courtesy GM Canada*

hardens on the surface of the plates, reducing their effective surface area and so effectively downgrading the capacity of the battery. If the level of the electrolyte falls below the top of the plates so that they become exposed to the air, this sulfation becomes more severe.

The life of a battery can be shortened by mechanical causes as well. Vibration can fracture the plates; posts can be torn out by their roots by ham-fisted attempts to disconnect a stuck terminal; and because the freezing temperature of the electrolyte rises rapidly as a battery becomes discharged, an

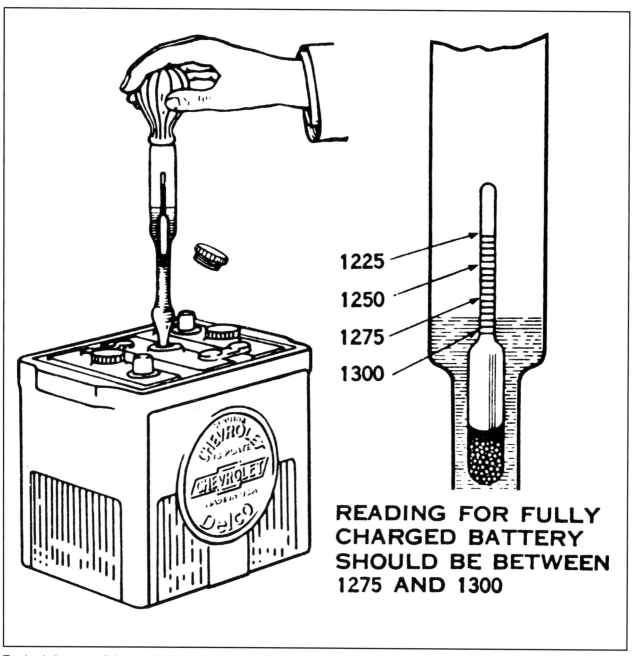

1225
1250
1275
1300

READING FOR FULLY CHARGED BATTERY SHOULD BE BETWEEN 1275 AND 1300

To check the state of charge of a battery with removable vent caps, a hydrometer is used. The float will ride at a certain height, according to the specific gravity of the electrolyte. *Courtesy GM Canada*

exhausted battery can freeze solid in cold weather, perhaps even splitting the case.

Recent developments in battery design have reduced the effects of many of these factors. New alloys for plate material, for instance, have greatly eased the problem of electrolyte boiling away, to the extent that the filler caps that used to be provided for topping up the cells with water are omitted from some "zero-maintenance" or "sealed-for-life" batteries. This also means that there is no risk of sedimentation from contaminated water.

Other recent developments include thinner cases and separators that leave more room for plates, so the amount of juice that a battery can store in relation to its bulk and weight is increased. Nevertheless, the energy-storage capacity of lead-acid batteries is still severely limited—which is why electric cars remain impractical, and why we need some means to constantly re-charge the battery.

Although a hydrometer shows the amount of charge remaining in a battery, it tells little about the condition of the plates and separators. On older batteries, a test meter could be used to measure the voltage of individual cells when loaded, by piercing the "tar-top" with a pair of electrodes.

Care of Stored Batteries

If you store your car for the winter, there are a few simple steps you can take that will greatly prolong the life of its battery. First, and most importantly, the battery should be fully charged. For this, a charger that operates at a small, fixed rate of 4 to 6 amps seems to work better than a "trickle" charger. Second, beware that a battery will gradually lose its charge during storage, and a partially discharged battery can freeze; if the case splits as a result, the battery is absolutely junk. (A fully-charged battery will withstand temperatures as low as minus 75 degrees; one that is half discharged will freeze at 10 below.) Third, the rate at which the battery self-discharges during storage slows down as the temperature drops—at 70 degrees a fully-charged unit will be down to a half charge after a couple of months, but at temperatures near freezing the rate of discharge will be so low that it will not need attention for several months. The ideal temperature for storage is 30 to 40 degrees. Fourth, the state of charge should be checked every month or six weeks, and the charger should be hooked back up whenever necessary. Finally, a battery with a hard rubber case should never be set on bare cement—it will self-discharge rapidly. Batteries with such cases should be set on a piece of wood; ones with plastic cases are not affected in this way. (And I will personally buy a beer for anyone who can explain to me why this is so!)

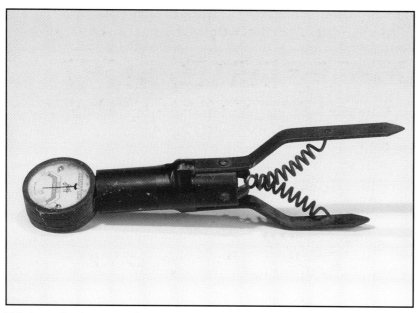

This is another instrument from the 1920s that would pierce the tar-top of an old battery to test it. Note the coiled resistance wire that provided the load.

CAUTIONS:

1. Never attempt to charge a frozen battery—it may explode!

2. Sulfuric acid is extremely corrosive; never allow battery acid to come into contact with skin. If it does, rinse it off immediately with large amounts of water. Acid in the eyes can cause almost instant blindness.

3. Highly flammable hydrogen gas is given off by batteries, especially when they are being charged; adequate ventilation must be provided. NEVER ALLOW OPEN FLAMES OR SPARKS NEAR A BATTERY, especially one that is being charged— not only is there a serious risk of fire, an explosion is possible, which can shower the surrounding area with sulfuric acid.

4. When disconnecting a battery, always unhook the ground cable first, to avoid accidentally creating a spark.

GET THE CUSTOMER STARTED RIGHT
Before installing a new battery or delivering a new car make certain that battery is fully charged.

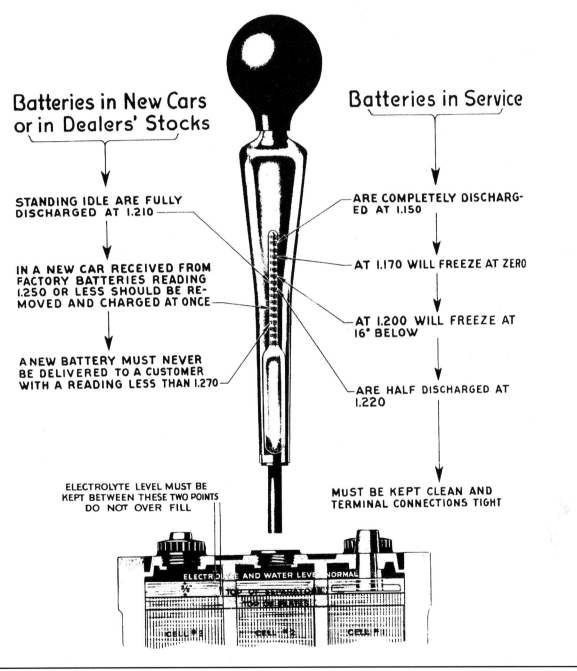

Batteries in New Cars or in Dealers' Stocks

STANDING IDLE ARE FULLY DISCHARGED AT 1.210

IN A NEW CAR RECEIVED FROM FACTORY BATTERIES READING 1.250 OR LESS SHOULD BE RE-MOVED AND CHARGED AT ONCE

A NEW BATTERY MUST NEVER BE DELIVERED TO A CUSTOMER WITH A READING LESS THAN 1.270

Batteries in Service

ARE COMPLETELY DISCHARG-ED AT 1.150

AT 1.170 WILL FREEZE AT ZERO

AT 1.200 WILL FREEZE AT 16° BELOW

ARE HALF DISCHARGED AT 1.220

MUST BE KEPT CLEAN AND TERMINAL CONNECTIONS TIGHT

ELECTROLYTE LEVEL MUST BE KEPT BETWEEN THESE TWO POINTS DO NOT OVER FILL

This Ford Service Bulletin explains how to test a battery with a hydrometer and also gives water levels and readings that were acceptable for a new battery. *Courtesy Ford Canada*

Generators, Alternators, and Regulators

3

The purpose of the generator or alternator is to replace the electricity we take out of the battery in order to run the starter motor. The regulator controls the output of the generator or alternator, to both protect the battery from harm through overcharging and to prevent the generator from damaging itself.

In the first chapter we noted that when a conductor cuts through a magnetic field, an electric current will flow in the conductor. The conductor has to be moving for this to happen, though, so it is necessarily a brief event. If the conductor stops moving, the current will cease to flow, and if it keeps moving, it will soon move out of range of the magnetic field. We can make this phenomenon repeat indefinitely, however, if we form the conductor into a loop or coil and then arrange for the coil to spin around close to the poles of a magnet, so that it keeps crossing and re-crossing the magnetic field.

If we did that, we would notice something else. As the conductor approaches one pole of the magnet (say north), the strength of the current will rise smoothly to some maximum value, then trail away. As it approaches the other (south) pole, the same thing will happen again, but this time the polarity will be reversed; if the first pulse of current grows from zero to some maximum positive value as the conductor makes its closest approach to the north pole and then diminishes smoothly to zero as it retreats, then the second one will start at zero and become more negative as it nears the south pole before trailing away to zero again as it withdraws. If we measured the current in the conductor and compared it to the rotational position of the coil, the result would look like the familiar sine curve.

AC and DC

Up to now, we have been describing current as water flowing through a pipe. Now, it is quite possible for water to flow either way through a pipe, but we're not accustomed to the idea that it might constantly change direction, flowing first one way, then the other. Our original simple model is for something called direct current (DC)—the juice always goes the same way. This new analogy, though, where the flow alternates between "forwards" and "backwards" is called alternating current (AC).

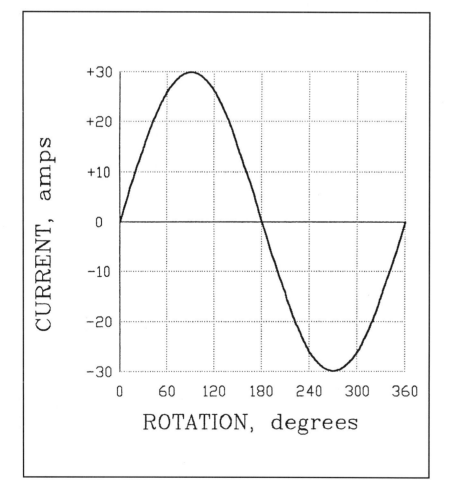

As a rotating loop or coil of conductor approaches a magnet, a current is produced in the conductor. The current rises to a peak as the conductor approaches, then reverses in polarity as the conductor retreats.

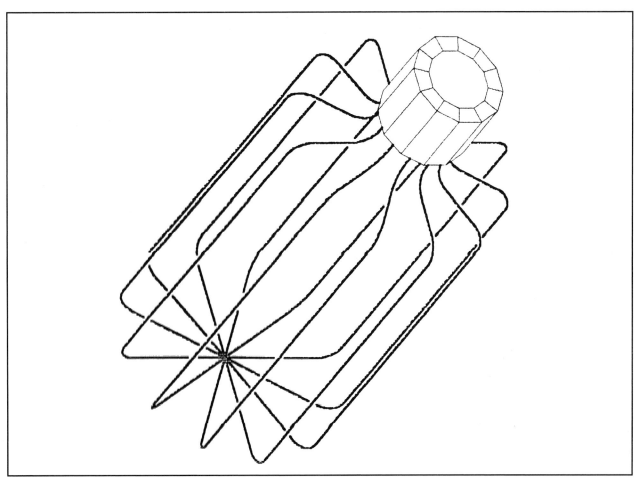

Multiple windings are used in any practical DC generator. To switch the polarity of the current in each coil before it has a chance to reverse, the coil ends are connected to a commutator, which is contacted by a pair of carbon brushes. The switching action of the rotating commutator "rectifies" the current—sorts it out so it always flows the same way.

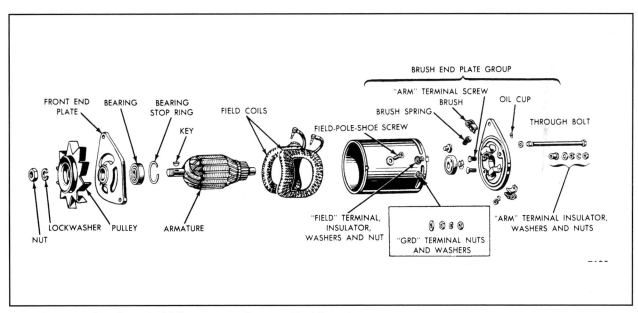

Internal construction of a typical DC generator. *Courtesy Ford Canada*

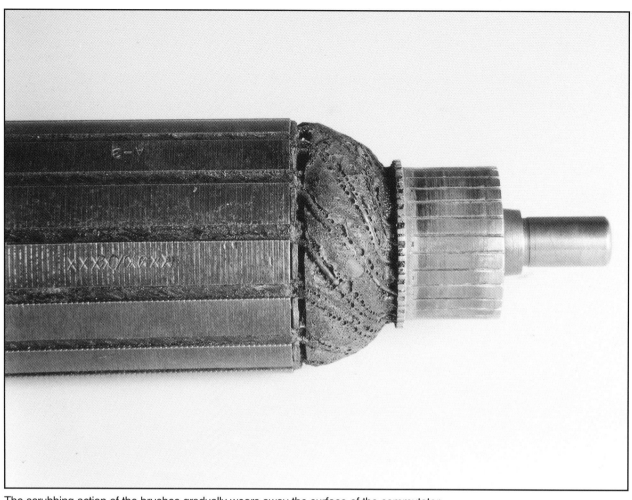

The scrubbing action of the brushes gradually wears away the surface of the commutator.

As you might imagine, this is no way to charge a depleted battery. If we were to hook up our rotating-coil-in-a-magnetic-field to a battery, the current would first flow into the battery, partly charging it, but then promptly turn around and flow back out again, discharging it by exactly the same amount. This is a problem that affects both generators and alternators, despite the fact that *generators* (as opposed to *alternators*) are often referred to as DC machines, which implies that they produce DC current. In fact, both generators and alternators actually produce AC, but they differ fundamentally in the way they convert the AC current to DC that can be used to recharge the battery.

DC Generators

In a DC generator, a sort of rotary mechanical switch called a commutator swaps around the terminals that connect with each end of the coil of conductor every half revolution. In other words, just as the current falls to zero, the connections are switched, so that just as the current is about to start to rise in the opposite direction, the coil itself is hooked up the other way around, so the next surge of current has the same polarity as the first. This means that the output of such a machine consists of a series of surges.

While an arrangement such as we have described would work, it wouldn't work very well. In practice, a generator is made with a large number of conduct-ing coils, arrayed at regular intervals around the central axis, and the commutator switches the output from one coil to the next every few degrees of rotation. That way, not only do we make better use of the bulk of the machine, the individual surges of current occur much more frequently, thereby smoothing the output to something much closer to pure DC.

In a real-world generator, the coils are formed over a steel core laminated from a large number of individual stampings, each of which looks like a gigantic star washer. This assembly is called the armature. Every coil is soldered, at each of its ends, to a small, roughly keystone-shaped piece of brass. Like the individual coils or loops, these segments are arrayed in a circle, separated from each other by an insulating material, such as mica. (Strictly speaking, the commutator is not part of the armature, but because the only way to separate them is with a hacksaw, the term "armature" is usually taken to mean the whole assembly of coils, steel core, and commutator, as well as the steel shaft that runs through the middle of the entire thing and to which the drive pulley and support bearings are mounted.)

To conduct the juice out of the commutator and to perform the switching function, there is a pair of stationary spring-loaded brushes made of carbon (another good conductor) that rub against the surface of the commutator.

Generators were last fitted to domestic cars in the 1960s, so any original generator is at least 30 years old and will sooner or later need attention.

Each brush contacts a commutator segment 180 degrees apart from the other, so as the armature is spun around by the fan belt, the brushes come into contact with successive pairs of commutator segments, one pair after another.

One final detail needs to be corrected in order to bring our description into line with reality. The magnets that provide the force field for the rotating loops of conductor to cut are not simple bar magnets. They could be, and some very small generators—as on bicycles—are made this way for the sake of economy and simplicity. But the magnetic field around most permanent magnets is not very strong, so the output of such a generator is poor in relation to its size and weight. To increase the output of the generators used in automotive applications, a stronger magnetic field is provided by electromagnets—separate coils of copper wire called field coils, wound around soft iron cores called pole pieces. The field

The rebuilt parts for a generator—here a 6-volt unit off a 1952 Chevrolet—include field coils, brushes, bushing for the brush end plate, ball bearing for the drive end, turned armature, plus small parts.

The complex internal wiring of a generator armature makes it difficult to check out, beyond the simple continuity checks mentioned in the text. For more comprehensive tests, some rather specialized equipment is needed, such as the "growler" seen here.

coils are energized (or "excited") by part of the generator's own output. (The pole pieces retain enough magnetism to allow the generator to begin making juice even when starting from a standstill, when there is no output to energize the field coils.)

Although the "DC" generator is a simple and, in some ways, elegant piece of engineering, it has a number of inherent problems. (We've put the "DC" in quotes because we've already seen that, internally at least, it doesn't really make DC at all.) First, the rubbing action of the brushes tends to

wear away both the brushes and, to a lesser extent, the commutator. As a result of the brushes wearing shorter, the spring tension that holds them against the commutator keeps getting weaker, which gradually affects output. Also, the brushes have to be replaced from time to time, and the commutator surface occasionally needs to be re-machined to smooth out the wear caused by the sliding action of the brushes. Further, the contact between the brushes and the commutator is by no means perfect, so considerable resistance is introduced at this

interface. What's more, the uneven surface of the commutator created by the alternating sections of brass and mica insulation tends to make the brushes bounce and chatter, further increasing the resistance. To compound these difficulties, the brush-to-commutator resistance gets worse as the speed increases, so any attempt to increase the output of the generator by turning it faster soon runs into a dead end. The rotational speed of a DC generator is also mechanically limited by the sheer mass of all that unsupported copper wire whirling around.

Charging-System Faults

While they all suffer from the problem of limited output at low speeds, generators are generally reliable machines. Nevertheless, it's worth remembering that they were last fitted to domestic cars in the 1960s, so any original generator is at least 30 years old and will sooner or later need attention.

The unmistakable clue that something is wrong with the charging system is its inability to charge the battery. Drivers of

> The unmistakable clue that something is wrong with the charging system is its inability to charge the battery. Drivers of cars with ammeters will get advance warning that the battery will soon be dead by the ammeter showing a discharge even when the engine is turning at a brisk clip.

cars with ammeters will get advance warning that the battery will soon be flat by the ammeter showing a discharge even when the engine is turning at a brisk clip and there is little electrical load. Even so, the problem could lie with the regulator rather than the generator, or there could be something constantly draining juice, or it could even be something as obvious as a broken fan belt.

If you determine that the drive belt is in place and that its tension seems about right, you can then determine if there is a hidden current drain someplace by disconnecting one of the battery cables—either one—and splicing an ammeter in between the battery post and the end of the disconnected cable. With the ignition and everything else turned off, there should be no amps flowing. If there is, it's time to start methodically checking every circuit to see if it's "live" when it shouldn't be, and working logically from there. Otherwise, there is surely something wrong with either the generator or the regulator.

To isolate the problem, splice an ammeter into the wire from the regulator that supplies the current to the generator's field coils and, with the engine running, measure the field current. If there is plenty of field current, the problem *must* lie with the generator. How much is "plenty" depends on the particular vehicle and on the state of charge of the battery. If the reason you're making this test is because the battery is too weak to turn the engine over, then on generator-equipped 12-volt systems you should expect to see an amp or two, or maybe even more on 6-volt vehicles. If there's no field current at all, then the problem very likely lies with the regulator.

Even if the electrical output of the generator seems satisfactory, the wearing parts—particularly the brushes—eventually need replacement. In most cases these are accessible without dismantling the whole shebang. Even if disassembly is necessary, this is a comparatively simple matter, and while you're inside, it is worth looking for and at other potential trouble spots.

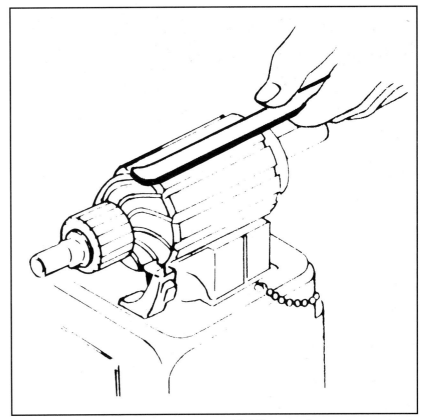

With the armature on the growler, a hacksaw blade is set on the armature segments to check for magnetism. If the blade is attracted, an armature coil is grounded to the armature frame. That's bad.

This simple lathe is used to machine the surface of a badly scored commutator.

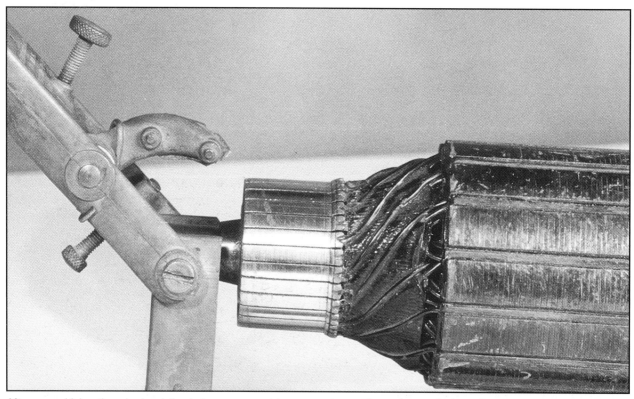

After re-machining, the mica insulation between commutator segments must be under-cut. A piece of hacksaw blade works, but this purpose-made tool does a faster and neater job.

Dismantling and Troubleshooting the Generator

With the unit off the car, first remove the cover plate that shields the brushes, and remove them. Next, remove the drive pulley. Then you have to dismantle the generator itself. Most generators are held together by two long screws that run the length of the casing. Once these are removed and the sections are pulled apart, you will be left with four main pieces—the cylindrical central body that holds the field coils, the drive end plate that contains an end bearing, the brush end plate with the brush holders, and the armature itself, which will probably just fall out as you separate the case.

Apart from the brushes and commutator, the point of greatest wear is usually the drive-end bearing, which may be either a ball bearing or a simple bushing. If a ball bearing is fitted, and it turns freely with no apparent lumpiness, it can be left

The Chrysler "round-back" alternator, introduced in 1960, solved the problems of DC generators by replacing the mechanical rectifier action of the commutator with diodes.

alone; if it is a bushing, you should figure it is junk and replace it as a matter of routine. In either case, the bearing or bushing can be pressed out of the end plate using a small puller or arbor press if you have one, or by the old "small socket, big-socket, and vise" technique. If original or reproduction replacement bearings or bushings are unavailable or are outrageously expensive, an industrial bearing supply house should be able to provide a generic replacement for just about any installation.

Inspect the inside of the case for signs of "thrown" solder. This indicates the generator has been seriously overheated at some point, and some of the solder used to connect the armature coils to the commutator has melted and centrifuged out into the case. This is a bad sign, and probably means the armature is seriously damaged. Otherwise, on Delco and other systems that ground the field coils through the regulator, check the field coils for

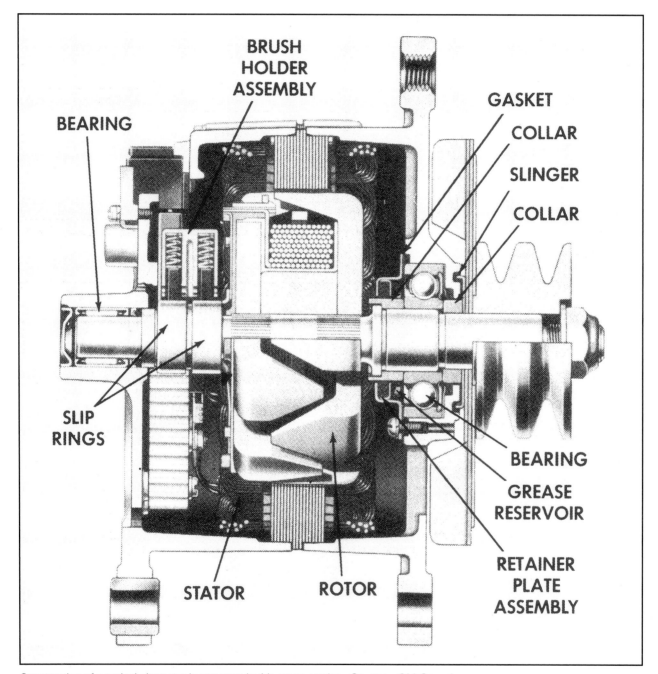

Construction of a typical alternator is apparent in this cross-section. *Courtesy GM Canada*

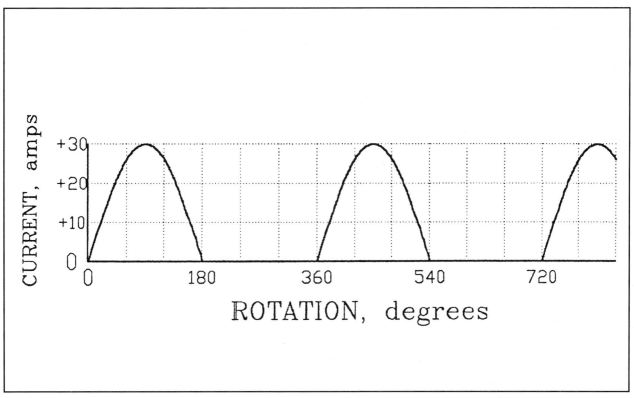

The one-way-valve action of a diode can be used to clip off the pulses of current going the "wrong" way, but this half-wave rectification wastes half of the alternator's output.

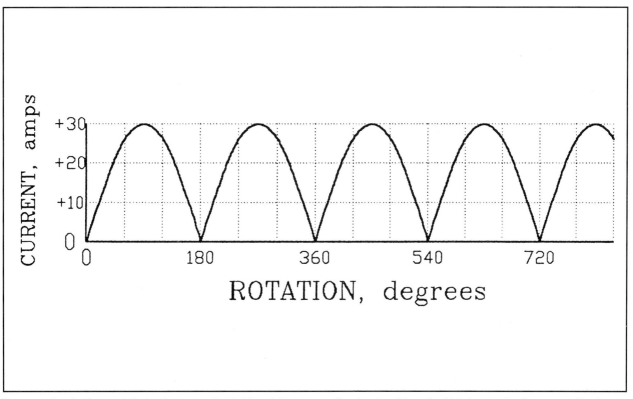

By arranging the internal diodes into a rectifier bridge, full-wave rectification is achieved, which inverts the "wrong-way" pulses.

grounds. Each coil should be electrically insulated from the case. Check the leads connecting the field coils to the brushes for broken wires and signs of rubbing. In the other end plate, check the brush holders and the springs for damage.

As to the armature itself, there are strict limits on what you can check out without special equipment. Certainly you can inspect the ends of the central shaft for mechanical damage and wear where they enter the end bearings. You can check for shorts by touching one probe of a multi-meter to the exposed end of the shaft, then touching the other probe to each commutator segment in turn; there should be no electrical path. Similarly, there should be no continuity between the armature and any commutator segment, though here the problem may just be caused by an accumulation of carbon dust from the brushes. If there is still continuity either place after you've carefully cleaned off any trace of black powder, there is an internal short and the armature is junk. You can also check that there is continuity between each commutator segment and the segment on either side of it; there should be. If there isn't, the problem may be visible—an armature winding that is broken or has come un-soldered from the commutator. You will have to judge for yourself whether it is worth attempting to fix this yourself, or whether you should leave the problem to a professional or simply obtain a replacement generator.

If the commutator is only glazed or lightly scored, you can clean up its surface with emery cloth or fine sandpaper, perhaps carefully jury-rigging an arrangement to spin the armature in a drill press. If you have access to a lathe, you can re-machine even a badly scored commutator. In either case, it is necessary to undercut the mica insulation between commutator segments after you're done. There are special tools made for this job, but it can be done with a broken piece of hacksaw blade. The idea is to clean away a little of the insulation so that it lies 0.030 to 0.060 inch below the surface of the commutator. You should reassemble the generator using new brushes, especially if the generator has to be dismantled to get at the brush-

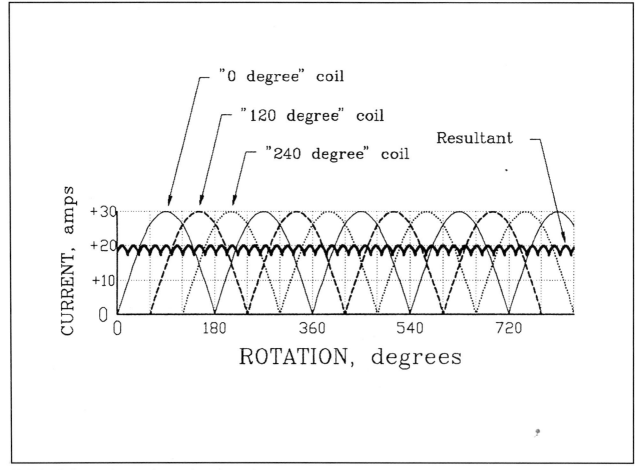

Multiple windings acting together produce a smoother output.

es. (If exact replacement brushes are hard to find, it is possible to slim down a set that is somewhat oversize by carefully rasping them on a piece of sandpaper set on a dead flat surface, such as a piece of plate glass.)

Alternators

The limitations of the DC generator were dealt with at one stroke with the introduction of the alternator. Chrysler was first, in 1960; other manufacturers soon followed suit. This new type of generator offered much greater output, especially at low speeds, and complete freedom from troublesome commutators, all in a lighter and more compact package. The secret was the use of

---

Even if the electrical output of the generator seems satisfactory, the wearing parts—particularly the brushes—eventually need replacement.

---

then-dawning solid-state technology, specifically a component called a diode—a kind of electrical one-way valve.

Like a traditional "DC" generator, an alternator produces AC; unlike a generator, the switching of the alternating current necessary to convert it to DC (a process called rectification) is achieved electronically, rather then mechanically. Because a diode only allows current to flow in one direction, a diode inserted

The mass of rotating metal within the armature distorts the magnetic field produced by the field coils, twisting it to a degree that depends on the speed of rotation.

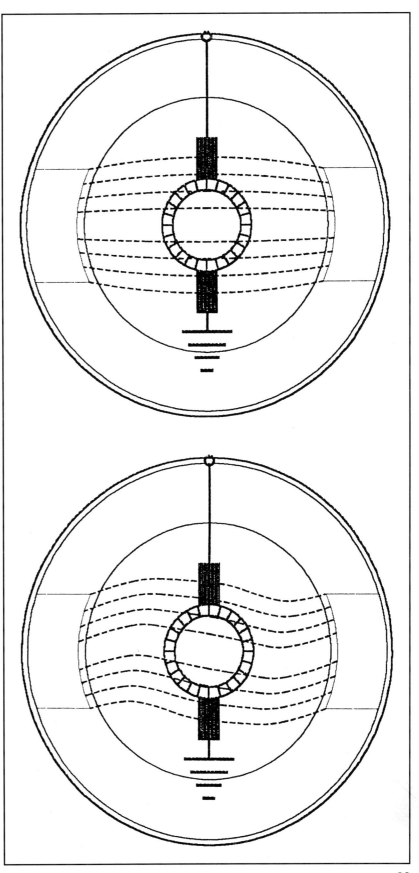

into the alternator's output circuitry blocks the "wrong" half of each cycle, yielding a pulsing form of DC. Smoothing out the pulses is achieved the same way as in a traditional DC generator—by the use of multiple sets of electromagnets and loops of conductors (called windings), though with a slight twist.

Compared to a generator, an alternator has its internal components turned inside out, so to speak: The heavier conducting coils are stationary, inside the fixed outer casing, while the lighter field coils (the electromagnets) rotate. The stationary collection of conducting coils is called the stator; the rotating assembly of field coils is called the rotor. The current necessary to excite the rotating field coils is fed into them by a set of brushes and slip-rings.

Although these slip-rings might seem to re-introduce the same problems as the commutator in a DC generator, there are two points to note. First, there are no segments on the slip-rings—the current flows in smoothly and continuously through one brush and slip-ring, through the stator's field coils, and back out again through a second brush and slip ring. The smooth, uninterrupted surface of the slip rings means that the rate of brush wear is very slow, and the problem of bounce and chatter is eliminated. Second, and more significant, the brushes only have to carry the comparatively small current required to excite the field coils in the rotor, not the full output of the machine, as is the case in a DC generator. For both these reasons, an alternator will often outlast the engine it's attached to, without any need for servicing.

There's nothing fundamentally different about the operating principle of an alternator—it's still a matter of a current-carrying conductor cutting through the lines of force of a magnet. Obviously, it doesn't matter whether the magnets stand still while the conducting coils move past them, or vice versa. This reversal of roles, however, permits the alternator to operate at much higher rotational speeds without excessive mechanical stresses.

Taking advantage of that higher speed rating by using a

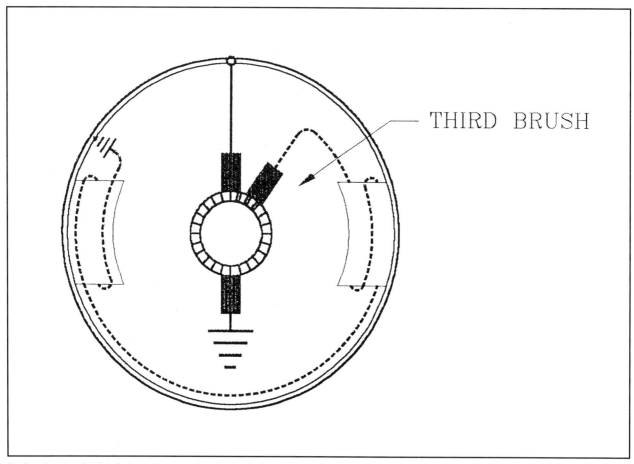

By feeding the field coils from an extra brush located some number of degrees around from the main current-collecting brushes, a "third-brush" generator achieves a degree of self-regulation.

different combination of driving and driven pulley sizes further enhances the alternator's low speed output; unlike a generator, an alternator can produce a useful amount of juice even when the engine is idling. About the only drawbacks to alternators are their somewhat larger external diameter compared to a generator of similar output (though the alternator is much shorter in the front-to-back dimension), and the sensitivity of the diodes to heat and to a "wrong-way" current that exceeds their ability to block.

If, for example, you connect jumper cables to an alternator-equipped car the wrong way around, you will very likely zap the diodes in the alternator.

Partly to smooth out the output surges, and partly to achieve mechanical balance, the rotor is wound with equally spaced electromagnet coils, in multiples of three. Each magnet coil induces into the stator coils the same rise and fall of current as the field coils of a generator produce in the armature. The output, measured at the stator,

resulting from the motion of one magnet varies according to the position of the magnets in the same sine-wave pattern we saw in connection with a DC generator. The diodes rectify (convert) this "hump-dip-hump" AC pattern into a "hump-pause-hump" form of pulsing DC.

Simply clipping off the "wrong-way" current would produce a series of widely spaced "humps." This half-wave rectification, as it is called, certainly prevents the current going the "wrong" way, but half of the out-

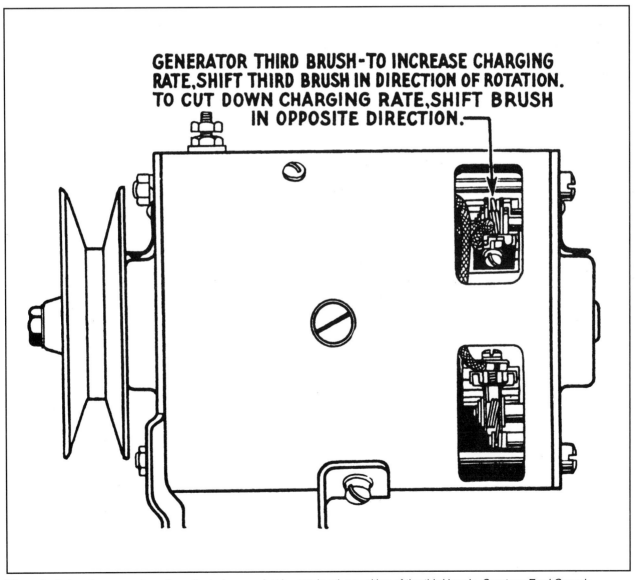

The output at a given speed can be adjusted somewhat by varying the position of the third brush. *Courtesy Ford Canada*

put of the coil—the "dips"—gets thrown away. To avoid this waste, and to provide a smoother output, the diodes are arranged in an array called a rectifier bridge, so as to convert the dips into humps. With this full-wave rectification, one hump immediately follows another.

When the separate rectified outputs of all the coils are superimposed on top of each other, the humps overlap and the result is something close to DC. (In truth, any component that might require *pure* DC—the computers used by modern engine management and other systems, for instance—would find this lumpy approximation unsatisfactory. Remember, though, that one of the functions of the battery is to smooth out variations in the electrical supply.)

Regulators

A battery will tolerate wide variations in the current that charges it, but it has its limits. We have already noted that excessive charging current or overcharging will reduce battery life; in extreme cases a battery can be quickly destroyed by this abuse. On the other hand, while a mere trickle of current will cause no harm, it will take ages for the battery to recharge. A simple generator as we have described above, however, has an output that grows with increasing speed, up to a point. What's needed, then, is some way to adjust the current being fed to the battery, according to its state of charge.

This was less of a problem 60 or 70 years ago, when the only electrical devices on a car were the starter, the ignition system, the headlights and taillamps, and maybe a horn. Under daytime operation, the only steady load was the small amount of

> Apart from the brushes and commutator, the point of greatest wear is usually the drive-end bearing.

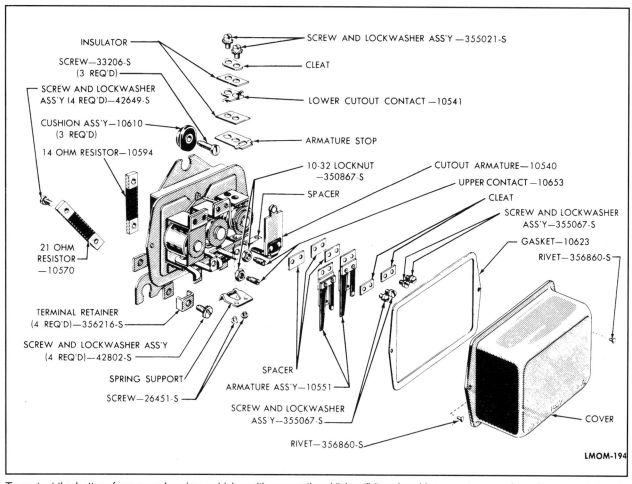

To protect the battery from overcharging, vehicles with conventional "shunt" (two-brush) generators need a voltage regulator. An electromagnet coil operates a set of contact points that rapidly switch the generator output on and off when the set voltage is reached, to limit the voltage fed to the battery. *Courtesy Ford Canada*

Voltage regulators use contact points that open as much as 200 times per second. Unlike contact points, the internals are tricky to service and replacement parts are difficult to find. *Courtesy Ford Canada*

juice needed by the ignition system, so generators for these cars did not need to provide much output—10 to 12 amps was sufficient. Regulation on these generators was through a system called a third brush.

The basis of the functioning of third-brush regulation is the fact that the lines of force between the field magnets become distorted by the presence of the rotating armature—they no longer run in straight lines from one pole to the other, but become twisted or skewed in the direction of rotation. The strongest part of the field, then, moves around somewhat, according to the speed of rotation. A third brush, strategically located, would pick up from the armature an amount of current that, with increasing armature speed, grows at first, but as the distortion of the magnetic field increases, the output tends to level off, then to decrease again. A certain amount of adjustment in the maximum output was made possible by

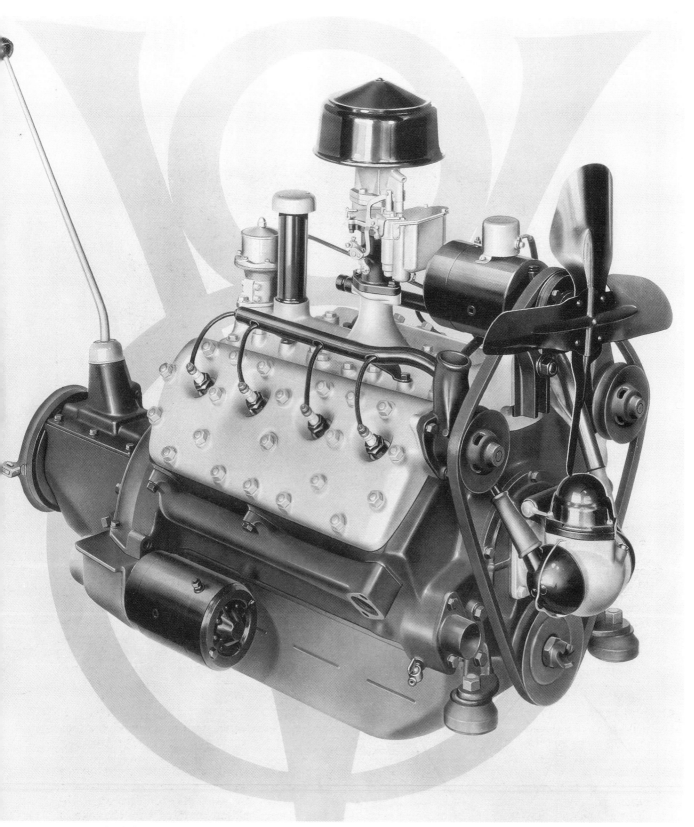

Self-regulating three-brush generators needed only a "cut-out" to prevent the battery from draining itself to ground through the generator brushes when the engine was stopped. It was often mounted right on the generator itself, as on this 1933 Ford flathead's generator. *Courtesy Ford Canada*

A third-brush-type Delco generator, used on many GM cars until the mid-1930s, also had the cut-out mounted on the generator.

allowing the third brush to be moved to various positions.

A refinement of third-brush regulation soon developed, to cope with the difference between daytime and night-time operation. Typically, a slightly larger generator was fitted, of perhaps 20 amps. When the headlights were off, a fixed resistance was switched in, to reduce field strength and so generator output. When the load of the lights was applied to the generator, this additional resistance was automatically cut out of the circuit by an extra set of contacts in the light switch.

Further elaboration of the automobile's electrical system, adding heater fans, windshield wipers, radios, and other

> Like a traditional "DC" generator, an alternator produces AC; unlike a generator, the switching of the alternating current necessary to convert it to DC is achieved electronically, rather then mechanically.

devices, demanded an increase in generator power to perhaps 30 amps, enough to seriously dam-

age the battery if it were not controlled. At the same time, the load might fluctuate much more widely as various accessories were turned on or off, so the simple two-step control provided by a switchable resistance would no longer suffice. Although the three-brush generator offers a means to control the current being fed to the battery, it requires someone to adjust it. Some form of automatic adjustment would be much better.

Conveniently, the rate of charge that a battery will tolerate without complaint is proportional to its degree of discharge—the closer to "flat" it is, the greater the charging current it will accept without harm. What's needed, then, is some way to adjust the current being fed to the battery, according to its state of charge. That's the job of the regulator, a device that began to appear in the middle 1930s, together with two-brush or "shunt" generators, a combination of equipment that remained pretty much unchanged until the introduction of alternators beginning in 1960.

Recall that both alternators and DC generators use electromagnets to provide the magnetic field that induces a current in the generating coils. Because the output of both types of generators depends on the strength of that magnetic field, a simple and convenient way to regulate the output is to vary the strength of the field by adjusting the current going through the electromagnets—the field coils in the case of a DC generator; the rotor windings in the case of an alternator.

Now, in order to stuff electrons back into the battery, the charging voltage has to be higher

---

Unlike a generator, an alternator can produce a useful amount of juice even when the engine is idling.

---

than the battery voltage. At the same time, the resistance offered by the battery is fairly constant over the usual operating range of state-of-charge, so the amount of charging current that will flow will depend on the applied voltage. From the point of view of the battery, then, the voltage is what we need to control.

The voltage regulator found on most older cars (ones with DC generators) consists of a spring, an electromagnet relay, and a set of contact points that act as a switch to turn on or off the juice flowing to the field coils in the generator. The spring initially holds the points in the closed (on) position, allowing the output from the generator's armature to energize its field coils. As the generator begins to spin, current starts to pass through the regulator's electromagnet coil. As the rotational speed of the generator increases and its output rises to, say, 13.5 or 14 volts (in a 12-volt system),

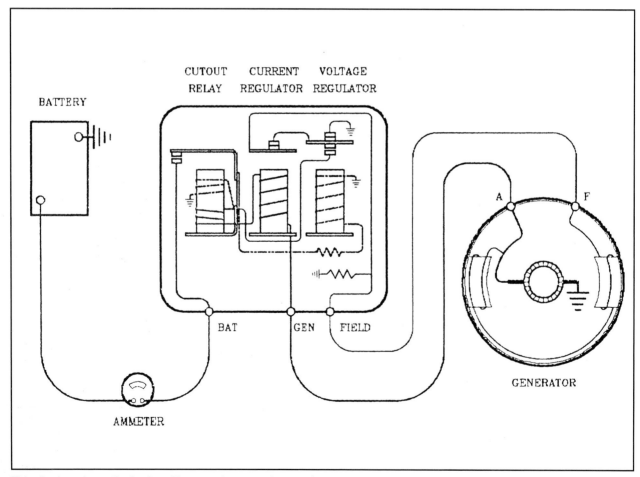

This diagram shows the basics of how a voltage regulator works.

Ross Reinhart of Antique Auto Electric uses a now-rare tool to adjust the settings on a three-coil Delco six-volt voltage regulator, as used from the 1940s through the middle 1950s.

enough current flows from the armature through the coil that the strength of the magnet exceeds the pull of the spring, so the magnet pulls the points open, interrupting the current flow to both the field coils and the relay. The current flowing through the relay therefore also stops, which turns off the electromagnet, allowing the points to close again.

This cycle repeats perhaps two hundred times per second, effectively regulating the output of the generator to the pre-set amount—slightly above the voltage measured across the terminals of a fully charged battery. Conversely, when the battery is discharged, its voltage drops considerably, so the same applied voltage from the generator will

> The voltage regulator found on most older cars consists of a spring, an electromagnet relay, and a set of contact points that act as a switch to turn on or off the juice flowing to the field coils in the generator.

result in a substantial flow of charging current into the battery. The battery's needs are thus fairly well satisfied.

While the battery may be kept happy by the voltage regulator, when the source of juice is a DC generator—as opposed to an alternator—there is another potential problem that needs to be prevented. Remember that virtually everything that uses electrical power in an automobile is designed to operate at the same voltage—whether 6 volts or 12. To achieve that, the separate components are wired in parallel. That means that every additional piece of equipment that gets turned on offers another path to ground, reducing the resistance the generator "sees." Since the voltage remains the same, increasing the electrical load, then, demands more current from the generator, and if the load is excessive, a DC generator can

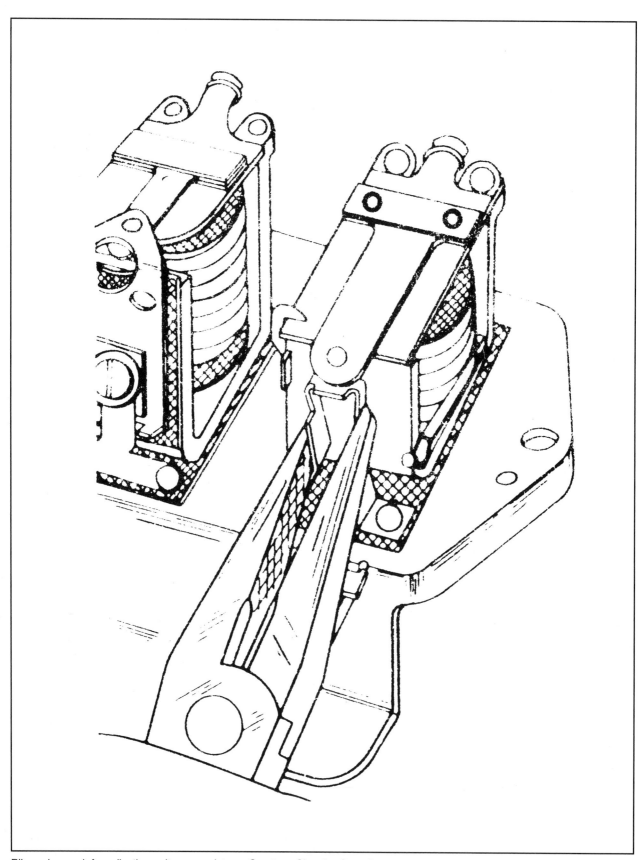

Pliers also work for adjusting voltage regulators. *Courtesy Chrysler Canada*

produce enough current to damage itself. For that reason, a current regulator is also incorporated into the regulator. It, too, comprises a set of points held open or shut by the balance of forces between a spring and an electromagnet coil.

Finally, to prevent the battery from draining back to ground through the generator when the engine is stopped, a third relay is provided, in addition to the voltage and current regulating functions. This cut out, as it is called, opens the circuit when the generator output is zero. (Even early three-brush generator systems used a cut out, for the same reason.) For convenience, these three separate functions are usually grouped together into one housing, and although only one of the devices actually regulates voltage, the entire business is called the voltage regulator.

Very little service is possible on a regulator. New points are almost never available to replace ones damaged by arcing, and in most cases you definitely should *not* attempt to clean up burned regulator contact points with a file or with emery cloth—tiny fragments of metal may fall into the rest of the works, causing a short, and the coating of (usually) tungsten on the surface of the contact points is extremely thin, so once it is gone, it is gone. (Some very early regulators had contact points made of solid chunks, rather than plated; these can be filed.) It is okay, and may sometimes be helpful, to clean the surface of the points by simply slipping a piece of paper between them and drawing it back and forth.

Also, while some early mechanical regulators have an adjusting screw for the voltage control contacts, most later ones do not, so the only way to compensate for springs that grow tired and upset the initial settings is to bend their mounting tags—a dicey business at best. In general, the technique is to measure the output of the generator without a load (i.e. not connected to the battery) and with the engine at a high idling speed, then to turn the adjusting screw (or bend the spring tab) at the voltage control relay until the points open at the correct value. This figure varies somewhat from make to make; somewhere around 14.2–14.5 volts is about

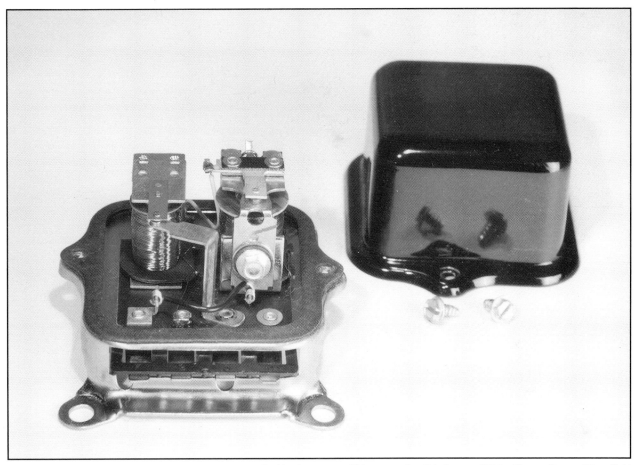

For a time, mechanical voltage regulators were used with alternators. This two-coil unit is from a 1960s Chevy. One coil is a field celay; the other is the voltage regulator.

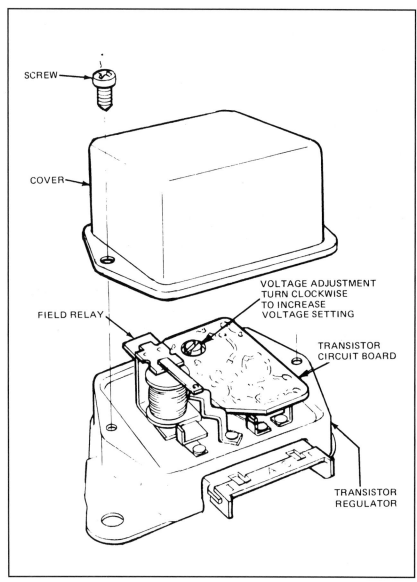

SCREW

COVER

FIELD RELAY

VOLTAGE ADJUSTMENT
TURN CLOCKWISE
TO INCREASE
VOLTAGE SETTING

TRANSISTOR
CIRCUIT BOARD

TRANSISTOR
REGULATOR

Even when voltage regulation began to be done electronically, a mechanical cut-out—here called a "field relay"—was sometimes retained. *Courtesy GM Canada*

the 1960s, though, many cars equipped with an alternator still used a mechanical regulator. Depending on the particular make and model of vehicle, a cut-out relay may also be included in the voltage regulator housing, but alternators do not suffer from the same risk of excess current that can fry a DC generator, so the mechanical regulators fitted to these vehicles do not include a current regulator. This freedom

> Very little service is possible on a regulator. New points are almost never available to replace ones damaged by arcing, and in most cases you definitely should not attempt to clean up burned regulator contact points with a file or with emery cloth—tiny fragments of metal may fall into the rest of the works, causing a short.

right for most 12-volt systems, 7.0–7.5 volts for a 6-volt system.

Because points can burn out and springs can corrode and become weaker with age, the traditional mechanical voltage regu-lator occasionally gives trouble. The same revolution in electronics that provided the diode soon made it possible to achieve volt-age regulation using solid-state devices. For a short period during

from the need for current regula-tion is yet another advantage of the alternator.

A point worth noting: The solid-state regulators in some modern alternators are set up to

The Chrysler mechanical voltage regulator used with an alternator between the introduction of alternators in 1963 and the appearance of solid-state regulators in the mid-1970s.

cope with "maintenance-free" batteries, which because of the different materials used for their plates, require a higher voltage to recharge than the older type. If such an internally-regulated alternator is fitted to a car having an old-fashioned, refillable battery, the battery will surely have its life shortened as a result of constant overcharging.

Another important point: Anytime the generator is removed or disconnected, the regulator should be re-polarized when the generator is re-connected and the battery hooked up, but before starting the engine. (This applies only to generator-equipped systems, not those with alternators.) To re-polarize the regulator on generator-equipped Fords (and any others that use an internal ground for the generator field coils), unhook the lead from the "Field" terminal on the regulator and briefly touch it to the "Bat" terminal. On Delco and other systems that ground the field coils through the regulator, briefly connect the "Bat" and "Armature" terminals.

This is the Chrysler solid-state regulator that replaces the mechanical unit in the previous illustration.

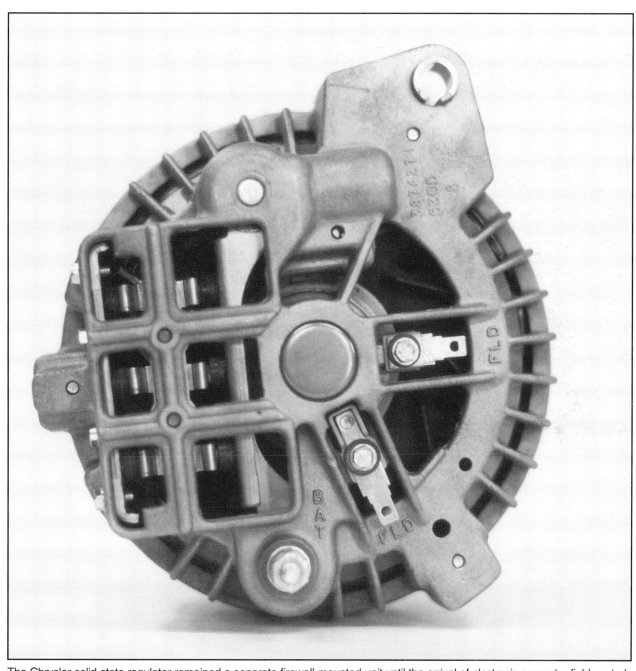

The Chrysler solid-state regulator remained a separate firewall-mounted unit until the arrival of electronic computer field control.

Starters, Starter Drives, and Relays

4

A DC electric motor looks exactly like a DC generator and has exactly the same internal components. Indeed, if you feed electrical power to a DC generator, it will turn of its own accord—it will act as a motor.

The same electrical effects are at work, too. Current fed to the field coils causes them to become electromagnets; current fed to the armature through the brushes and commutator causes the particular coil or coils that

are excited to become magnets themselves. If the polarities are arranged so that the armature winding near the north field pole is itself north, it will be repelled away from the field. Since the only way it can escape is to turn

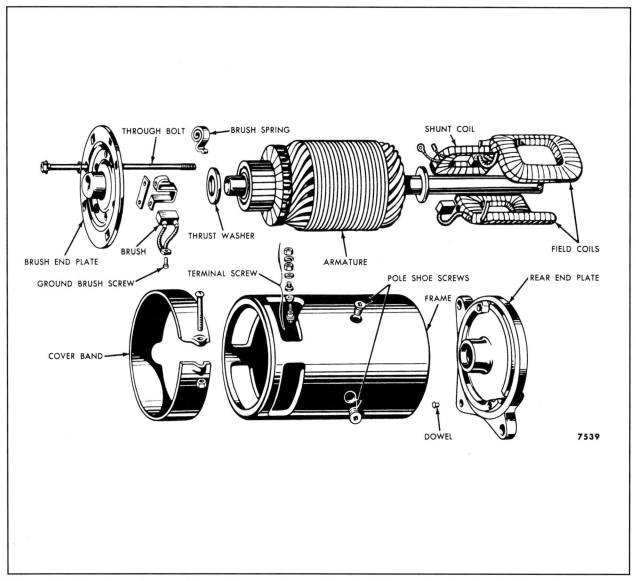

This exploded view shows the resemblance between a starter motor and a DC generator. *Courtesy Ford Canada*

the armature, the armature is forced to rotate. As that winding moves away from the influence of the field, the commutator switches the current to the next winding, and it too is pushed away, and so on. Meanwhile, the same thing has been going on between the south field coil and the other half of the energized loop of conductor, which acts like a south pole.

(It's worth noting that there are now some permanent magnet DC motors in a few automotive accessory applications. These use magnets made from rare metallic elements that can retain a much stronger magnetic field than plain old iron; the saving in copper for the field coils and the obviously simpler construction more than offset the extra cost of the magnet material in some applications. You won't find any of these on cars of the era we are discussing, unless you put them there yourself, but if you should do so, you should know that a permanent magnet motor will run backwards if you reverse the polarity! Since permanent magnet motors have only appeared in automotive applications very recently—long after the automotive world standardized on 12-volt systems with negative grounds—this will only be an issue if you have an unconverted 12-volt *positive-ground* car.)

It takes somewhere between 1 1/2 and 3 horsepower to crank an automobile engine up to the speed where it will run by itself. Since 1 horsepower equals 746 watts, that means a 12-volt

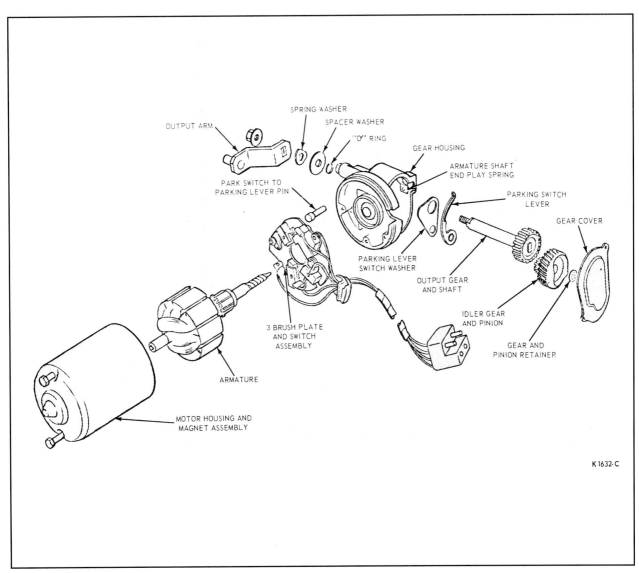

The similarity between DC motors and DC generators extends to the occasional use of third-brush motors. The two speeds of this windshield wiper motor are achieved by feeding current to either the main or third brushes. *Courtesy Ford Canada*

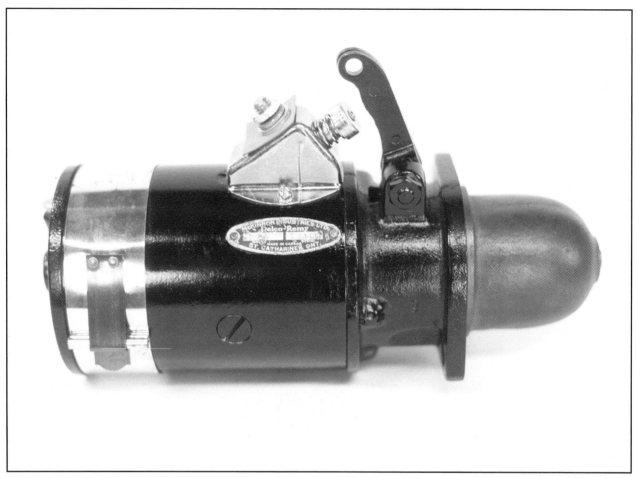

Among the simplest ways to engage the starter pinion and turn the current on at the same time is seen on this GM starter motor used in the 1930s and 1940s. A foot pedal pulls on the protruding lever, which first meshes the pinion, then closes the switch controlling the juice.

starter will need to draw somewhere between 100 and 200 amps to make that sort of power; a 6-volt unit will demand twice as much. By automotive standards, that is a lot of current—by far the largest single demand made on an automobile's electrical system. It is also several times the current that an automotive DC generator can produce, so not only are the windings in a starter motor much huskier than those in a generator, it is also common to find four brushes in starter motors, rather than two, for the same reason.

Starter Drives
In the earliest days of electric starting, there were a few

It takes somewhere between 1 1/2 and 3 horsepower to crank an automobile engine up to the speed where it will run by itself. Since 1 horsepower equals 746 watts, that means a 12-volt starter will need to draw somewhere between 100 and 200 amps to make that sort of power.

attempts to combine the functions of starter and generator in one package. In some cases this combination unit, called a dynamotor, was mounted directly to the crankshaft, so there was no gear reduction between the electric machine and the engine. Because of the high torque necessary to turn over a cold engine, these apparatus were very large in diameter, very heavy, and demanded a huge amount of current to successfully spin the engine when in starter mode. This principle survived into the 1960s, and perhaps even later, on some of the very small engines used in micro-cars such as the Isetta, where the "scale effect" made it practical.

50

To prevent the engine from overspeeding the engaged pinion, a one-way roller clutch may be used.

For larger engines, though, some amount of gear reduction is necessary to obtain sufficient torque to turn the engine over without demanding a starter that weighs as much as the engine itself. Other efforts to merge the generating and starting functions on realistically sized engines either employed a gear ratio between the armature and the engine crankshaft of about 2:1—which still left the whole business inconveniently large and also spun the generator/starter dangerously fast at high engine speeds—or else used a driver-controlled two-speed

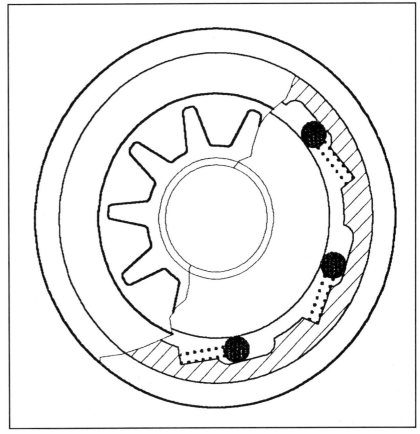

When the starter motor drives the pinion, the rollers ride up the ramp-shaped cams inside the clutch, which locks the armature shaft to the pinion. When the engine attempts to drive the mechanism in reverse, the rollers get driven down the ramps, disconnecting the drive.

transmission of some sort to give a low ratio when generating and a high one for starting. All of these oddball arrangements were obsolete by the late 1920s. The hope to simplify things by using just one electric machine was recognized as futile, and separate generators and starters were installed, which allowed each to have an optimum speed ratio relative to the engine.

To get the leverage necessary for a compact starter to turn over a stationary engine, a suitable gear ratio between it and the crank is generally somewhere between 10:1 and 15:1, and for the last 70 years or more this has been achieved by a small gear—the "pinion"—on the end of the starter motor armature that meshes with the much larger ring gear mounted on the engine's flywheel. However, for the reasons hinted at above, the starter pinion cannot be left permanently engaged with the ring gear. While the starter may spin the engine up to a few hundred rpm to start it, the engine can run at several thousand rpm; if the starter pinion stayed engaged in the ring gear, the starter would be spun around at tens of thousands of rpm when the engine is running at normal speeds, destroying the starter.

In general, what's wanted is to have the pinion engaged when the power to the starter motor is turned on, and pulled out of mesh when the electrical power is off. Various ways have been devised to ensure that these two functions—the physical movement of the pinion and the electrical switching—take place

The coarse "translation" thread and lop-sided weighting of the pinion that form the basis of the Bendix or inertial starter drive are visible here.

together. Among the simplest methods is to provide a pedal-operated linkage that, first, mechanically pushes the pinion into mesh, then, as the linkage nears the end of its travel, closes a pair of electrical contacts that turns on the juice. This kind of arrangement was used through the 1930s and 1940s on GM vehicles. To allow for the brief moment after the engine fires but before the driver has responded by letting off the pedal, an overrunning or one-way clutch is fitted to the end of the starter shaft, so the starter can drive the pinion, but the pinion can't drive the shaft.

> During the 1920s and 1930s, the Bendix drive was probably the most common form of connection between starter and engine.

An alternative method of synchronizing the electrical and mechanical switching is the Bendix drive, which provides an automatic means to engage the pinion when the starter motor is spinning, and to disengage it after the engine fires. The principle is quite simple. The end of the starter-motor shaft is provided with a very coarse male thread, and the pinion has a corresponding female thread. When the power to the starter motor is turned on and it suddenly begins to spin, the inertia of the pinion

Use of a barrel sleeve to contain the mating female threads allows the pinion to be made smaller, for a better reduction ratio, without dangerously slimming the shaft. Translation threads are clearly visible here.

ILLUSTRATIONS OF VARIOUS TYPES OF BENDIX STARTER DRIVES
AND REFERENCE TO TECHNICAL SERVICE BULLETIN COVERAGE

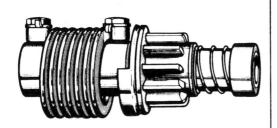

SCREW TYPE (Bulletin DR-1)

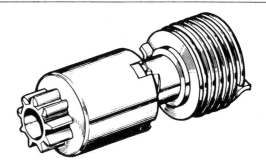

BARREL-ANCHOR PLATE (Bulletin DR-2)

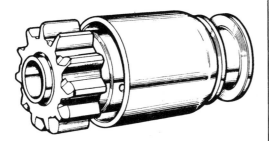

POSITORK (Bulletin DR-3)

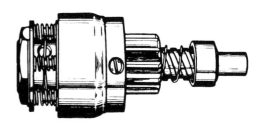

FRICTION CLUTCH (Bulletin DR-4)

RUBBER FOLO-THRU (Bulletin DR-5)

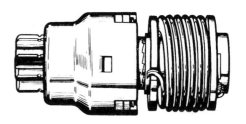

SPRING FOLO-THRU (Bulletin DR-5)

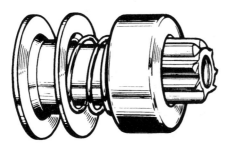

ROLLER CLUTCH (Bulletin DR-6)

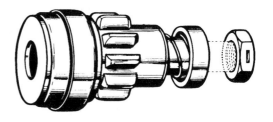

RUBBER COMPRESSION (Bulletin DR-7)

Bendix drives come in a wide assortment of types. *Courtesy GM Canada*

tends to make it lag behind, so it whizzes down the thread and into mesh with the ring gear. (The pinion is sometimes made deliberately unbalanced, to help this effect.) When the motor fires and begins to drive the pinion faster than the starter motor is going, the pinion screws itself back along the shaft the opposite way, and so out of engagement with the ring gear.

As just described, there is the problem that the starter motor is running at a good clip when the pinion becomes engaged, and the violent shock that would occur when it encounters the stationary flywheel risks shredding teeth off the ring gear, or other mechanical damage. To avoid this severe jolt, a refinement is introduced. Rather than the pinion itself being screwed along the motor shaft, a separate threaded collar acts as the "nut," connected to the pinion via a strong coil spring that helps to cushion the blow. (Despite this extra feature, starter engagement is quite a violent event. Early Ford starters, for example, in which the pinion are overhung without an extra support bearing at the outboard end, are prone to bending of the starter shaft, especially if an original 6-volt starter is run on 12 volts.) An additional refinement was the inclusion of a detent that tended to latch the pinion in position once it had fully meshed with the ring gear. Without this feature, the slightest cough from the engine will tend to spit the pinion out of engagement; the pinion will chatter in and out of mesh without ever getting the engine up to a speed where it will continue to run. During the 1920s and 1930s, the Bendix drive was probably

A starter relays from a 6-volt-era Ford. Note that there is only one primary terminal (the unit grounds through its mounting bracket). In 1950, the mounting was insulated, so there were two primary terminals.

Like the earlier of the two Ford starter relays in the previous illustration, this six-volt unit from a 1951–54 Chevrolet apparently has only one primary terminal; the "invisible" second primary connection is the mounting bracket. The comparative sizes of the secondary terminals and the primary suggest how impractical it would be to switch the starter current directly, using a dash-mounted switch.

the most common form of connection between starter and engine.

An advantage of the Bendix drive is that the movement of the pinion is an automatic, mechanical result of the electrical power to the starter being turned on. The only thing the driver's control (lever or pedal) needs to operate is the electrical switching. This simplifies turning the operation into a true push-button affair—all that's needed is a relay to switch the large current flow to the starter, a technique Ford employed from 1949 through the end of the 6-volt era.

Starter Relays

To avoid excessive voltage drop, and so give the starter motor all the juice it needs, the cables carrying the current to the starter need to be both short and fat. Likewise, whatever does the switching of that much current has to be equally husky. To avoid having a starter switch in the dashboard that is the size of a pop can, and to avoid a length of cable as thick as your thumb running from the battery to the dash, and back to the starter motor, it is convenient to switch the starter current through a relay.

A relay is a type of electrical switch that uses a small current to control a large one—to "relay" the message, in other words. It consist of an electromagnet energized by the small current to pull a plunger. The plunger, in turn, bridges a pair of stout contacts to turn on the big juice. This arrangement allows the relay to be mounted on or near the starter, keeping the main current-carrying conductors short, while a much smaller wire carries the "signal" current between the key switch and the relay.

This interior view of the Chevrolet relay shows the large copper contacts that switch the hefty current going to the starter.

At this point it is appropriate to talk about the difference between a relay and a solenoid. The same electromagnetically produced plunger movement that provides a switching action in a relay can also be used for other purposes. It is used, for example, to physically move the door locks in a central locking system. When it is the physical motion that is desired, the device is called a solenoid. In other words, a relay is a solenoid whose mechanical movement is used to actuate a switch. It is also possible for a solenoid to serve as a mechanical actuator and as an electrical switch at the same time, and many starters use a solenoid in that way. Here's why.

Since we want the pinion engaged only when the starter is cranking, and disengaged at all

> To avoid excessive voltage drop, the cables carrying the current to the starter need to be both short and fat.

other times, it is often convenient to use a "solenoid relay" (that's what Buick called it in the Dynaflow era) mounted right on the starter motor both to switch the starter current *and* to move the pinion into mesh. GM and Chrysler products have used this arrangement for a number of years.

The solenoid, mounted on the top of the starter motor, tugs

on one end of a lever; the lower end of the lever has a forked shape that fits over a collar attached to the pinion. The pinion is splined to the armature shaft so it must turn when the armature turns, but it is free to slide lengthwise. When the solenoid is energized by the key switch, the electromagnetic attraction first pulls the plunger toward the coil, swiveling the lever, and so shoving the pinion into mesh. When it reaches the end of its travel, the plunger bridges across a pair of contacts, turning on the starter motor. Once the engine is started and the key switch is released, a strong spring returns the plunger to its rest position, switching off the motor current and pulling the pinion out of mesh. To deal with the brief

57

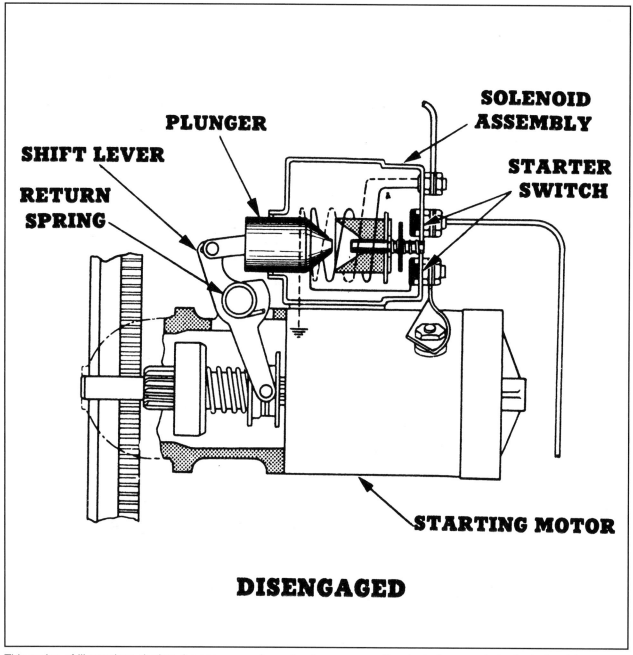

PLUNGER

SHIFT LEVER

RETURN SPRING

SOLENOID ASSEMBLY

STARTER SWITCH

STARTING MOTOR

DISENGAGED

This series of illustrations depicts the sequence of events when a conventional, starter-mounted relay/solenoid operates. Here, the system is shown at rest. The solenoid coil has no current flowing through it and the pinion is held out of mesh with the flywheel by a return spring. *Courtesy of General Motors Canada*

moment after the engine fires, but before the key is released, an overrunning clutch is provided.

(Modern Fords do things a little differently. They, too, and for the reasons noted above, use a relay to switch the main starter current, but Ford relays are mounted on the firewall, as they always have been; the engagement and disengagement of the pinion is achieved by a rather oddball arrangement in which one of the starter motor pole shoes—the iron cores in the center of the field coils—is free to slide lengthwise. When the relay is energized and turns on the juice to the starter motor, this sliding pole shoe slides the pinion into engagement with the ring gear through a lever arrangement similar to the one described above.)

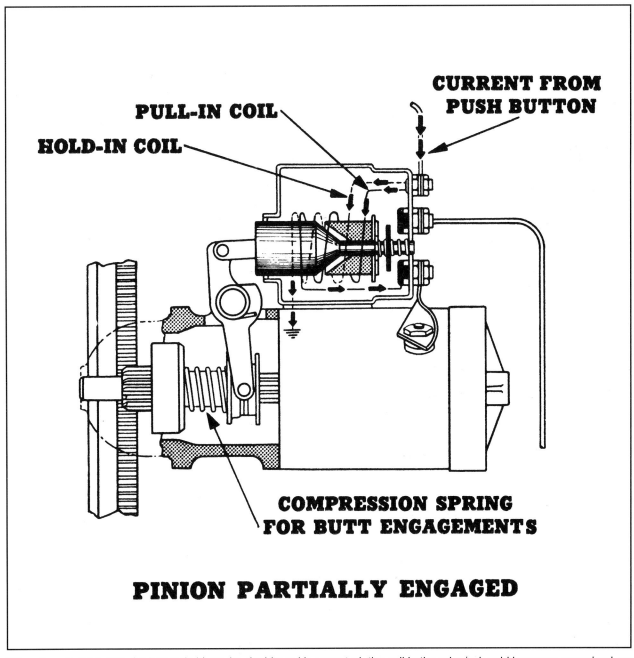

PULL-IN COIL

HOLD-IN COIL

CURRENT FROM PUSH BUTTON

COMPRESSION SPRING FOR BUTT ENGAGEMENTS

PINION PARTIALLY ENGAGED

When the starter button (or key switch) on the dashboard is operated, the coil in the relay/solenoid becomes energized, so the core becomes an electromagnet.

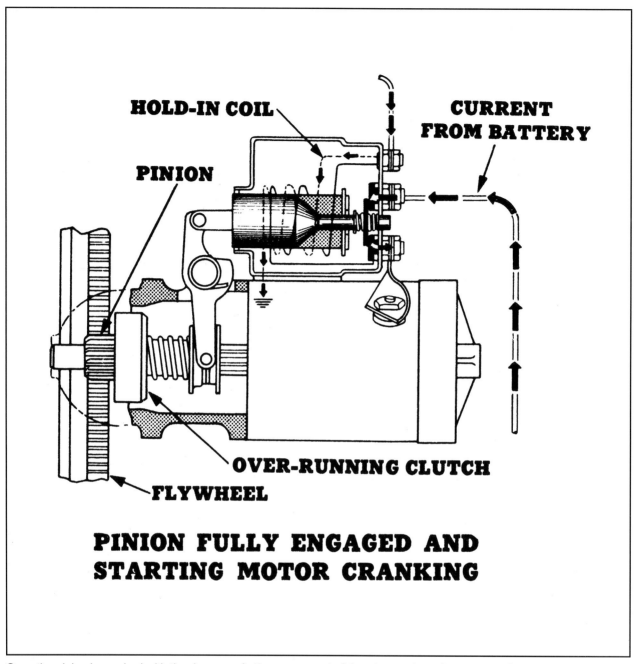

HOLD-IN COIL

PINION

CURRENT FROM BATTERY

OVER-RUNNING CLUTCH

FLYWHEEL

PINION FULLY ENGAGED AND STARTING MOTOR CRANKING

Once the pinion is meshed with the ring gear, further movement of the plunger then closes a set of contacts to turn on the current to the starter motor itself. When the driver releases the dash switch, the current through the relay coil is interrupted, allowing the return spring to pull the pinion back out of engagement. *Courtesy General Motors Canada*

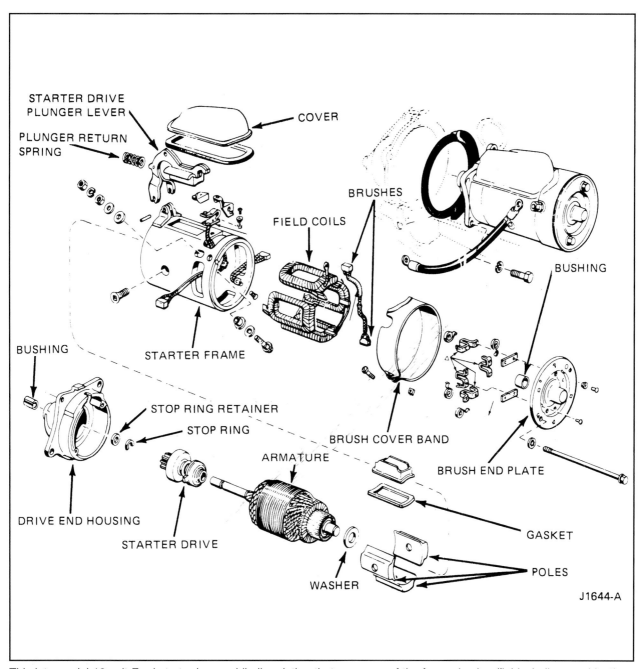

STARTER DRIVE
PLUNGER LEVER

PLUNGER RETURN
SPRING

COVER

BRUSHES

FIELD COILS

BUSHING

BUSHING

STARTER FRAME

STOP RING RETAINER

STOP RING

BRUSH COVER BAND

ARMATURE

BRUSH END PLATE

DRIVE END HOUSING

STARTER DRIVE

GASKET

POLES

WASHER

J1644-A

This late model 12-volt Ford starter is an oddball variation that uses one of the four-pole shoe/field winding combinations as a solenoid. When the topmost of the illustrated field coils is energized, the magnetic field around it forces the pole shoe to slide endwise. That motion acts through the plunger lever, pushing the drive pinion into mesh with the flywheel ring gear. *Courtesy Ford Canada*

This cutaway illustration of a 1939 Ford flathead starter motor show typical construction details of the brush end of the motor. Note, however, that there is no separate sleeve covering the brushes; to inspect or replace the brushes, it is necessary to remove the end plate. The hefty coil spring used to reduce the engagement shock of this Bendix-type starter is conspicuous at the opposite, drive end. *Courtesy Ford Canada*

Ignition Systems

5

The modern car is about as reliable as a fridge, and requires only slightly more maintenance. Apart from an oil and filter change every presidential election, they seem to run almost forever with no attention whatsoever. Yet until quite recently—say, within the past decade or so—every car owner accepted that, as time went by, performance would begin to fade, fuel mileage would worsen, and starting would become more difficult and less certain, especially in cold weather. The only way to set right this deterioration was to replace the points, condenser, and spark plugs; less often, a new distributor cap and/or rotor were needed; and once in a while the list of new parts extended to the coil and high-tension ignition wiring.

As the above list shows, and as any car person old enough to remember the Cold War knows, most of what was called a regular tune-up consisted of replacing ignition-system components, a process that sometimes needed to be repeated as frequently as two or three times a year. Though none of the operations involved in these tune-ups was beyond the capabilities of a methodical amateur, garage operators everywhere made a good part of their living from the profit on these parts, and on the labor billed to change them.

While no purchaser of a new car these days would tolerate this routine, an earlier generation of drivers took it for granted. They had learned from their fathers (and their fathers had learned from *their* fathers) that this was as much a part of what is today called "the ownership experience" as the need to pour gas in the tank. It was routine stuff, taken for granted, like the need to take showers and brush your teeth. This attitude amounted to an acceptance that the ignition system was, and always had been, the Achilles' heel of the gasoline engine. Indeed, the absence of a troublesome ignition system, and freedom from the need for regular ignition tune-ups, was sometimes even touted as an argument for diesels!

Most of what was called a regular tune-up consisted of replacing ignition-system components, a process that sometimes needed to be repeated as frequently as two or three times a year.

In most of the very earliest internal-combustion engines—gigantic single-cylinder stationary power plants, running on natural gas or coal gas—ignition was by means of a "hot-tube" igniter. The tube, made of porcelain, or sometimes platinum, was located immediately outside the combustion chamber, and was continuously heated by a small gas flame that made it glow red hot. As the piston approached top center on the compression stroke, a timing valve opened, operated by a cam or crank-and-rod mechanism, exposing the contents of the combustion chamber to the hot tube, which lit (sometimes) the combustible mixture in the cylinder. Amazingly, this arrangement was also used in some very early automobiles; accounts written around the turn of the century make reference to frequent stoppages resulting from the flame blowing out!

What may be more amazing is that this primitive scheme replaced some electrical ignition systems that had actually been used even earlier. Lenoir's gas engine of 1861, the first commercially-produced internal-combustion engine, used an electric spark to light the fuel-air mixture, as did the first successful car, the Benz automobile of 1885.

Perhaps the unwillingness of early car and engine makers to embrace electrical ignition was attributable to the same hesitation concerning electrical apparatus that unnerves contemporary mechanics and restorers. Whatever the source of this initial reluctance, by the early 1900s the days of hot-tube ignition were over, and the automotive world followed the lead shown earlier by Benz and Lenoir.

As is common with emerging technologies, there was a bewildering proliferation of designs at first. For all the variety, though, there were really only two general categories: magnetos of various types and systems based on an induction coil. Magnetos eliminated the need for a battery—in those days a fragile device, and even heavier than those of today—and so became almost universal for use on race cars, motorcycles, and aircraft. Induction-coil systems

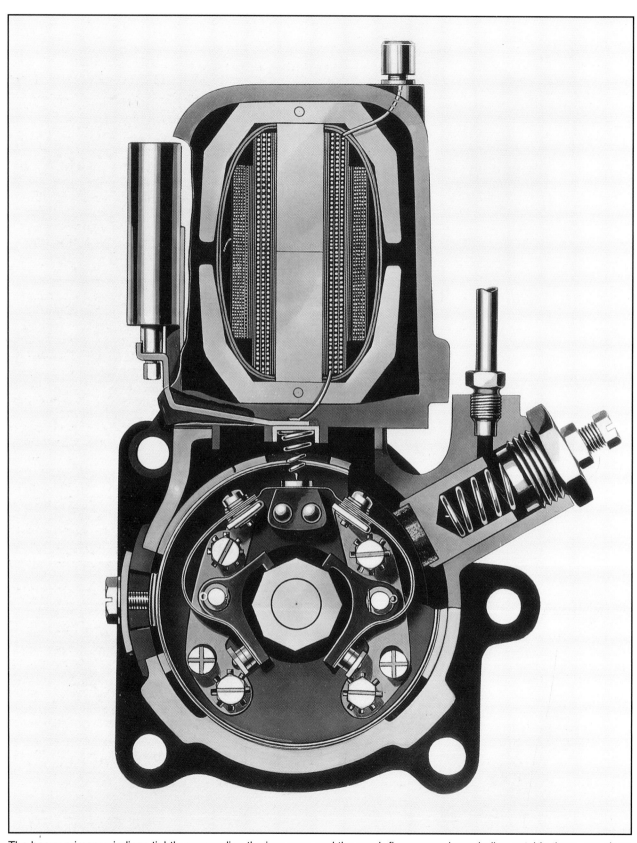

The heavy primary windings tightly surrounding the iron core, and the much finer secondary winding outside them, are clearly seen in this cutaway view of a 1939 Ford coil. *Courtesy Ford Canada*

offered an advantage over magnetos—improved ignition at low speeds—but required an onboard source of low voltage, typically a battery. However, as electric lighting (and, later, electric starting) became widespread, the battery was seen as less of a liability, and design rapidly converged toward the coil-and-breaker system designed in 1911 by Charles Kettering (who also invented the electric starter). This Delco system—named after the Dayton Electric Company, founded by Kettering—rapidly became almost universal after its introduction on GM cars in 1922, and remained so for more than half a century.

Coil and Breaker Ignition

In construction, an induction coil is not complex. It consists of a central core of soft iron surrounded by two separate windings of copper wire. One of the windings, called the primary, consists of a small number of turns (typically a couple of hundred) of comparatively thick wire; the other, called the secondary, consists of a much larger number of turns of much finer wire. At one end, the primary winding is connected to the hot lead of the electrical source, almost always a battery; the other end is grounded, at least most of the time. The secondary winding shares the primary's connection to the hot lead of the battery; the other end is connected to the spark plug's center electrode (though in the case of an engine with more than one cylinder, this connection is likely to be indirect, via the distributor cap and rotor, as we shall explain).

When current flows through the primary winding, a magnetic field is created in the core, and this field is maintained as long as current is flowing. But if this flow then suddenly stops for any reason, say by a switch being opened, the magnetic field in the core collapses, and the stored magnetic energy "induces" a burst of electricity in the secondary winding—hence the name "induction coil." The interruption of the current flow is accomplished by the breaker "points" that consists of a pair of contacts, normally held closed by a spring, but which are pushed open at the appropriate time by a rotating cam. The cam is driven at half of crankshaft speed, since a spark is only required every second crank revolution on a four-stroke engine.

It's worth mentioning here that the voltage in the secondary winding of the coil will only rise as high as it has to in order to jump the spark plug gap. Talk of systems or coils with zillions of volts output is pure hype: Under most circumstances, the secondary voltage is somewhere around 10,000 volts or less.

While the primary circuit nominally operates at just 6 or 12 volts, the induced secondary voltage is a thousand or more times higher than that—sufficient to jump the gap in the spark plug. Usually this conversion from low voltage to high is explained as being a result of the difference in the number of turns in the two windings, just as an ordinary household transformer multiplies voltage. In fact, although an induction coil is *built* like a transformer, and although the same electrical symbol may be used for both, an induction coil does not *work* just like a transformer.

The high voltage in the secondary circuit when the primary is interrupted has comparatively little to do with the "turns ratio" of the coil, but has everything to do with the speed with which the field in the core collapses—the faster this occurs, the higher the voltage. More to the point, the collapse of the core's field induces a high voltage in both the secondary *and* the primary circuits. The relative voltages in the two does depend on the turns ratio, however, so while the voltage in the secondary circuit may rise to 10,000 volts or more, the primary circuit momentarily experiences a surge of perhaps a couple of hundred volts. (It's worth mentioning here that the voltage in the secondary winding of the coil will only rise as high as it has to in order to jump the spark plug gap. Talk of systems or coils with zillions of volts output is pure hype: Under most circumstances, the secondary voltage is somewhere around 10,000 volts or less. Besides, if you were to force a coil capable of, say, 50,000 volts to actually rise that high—say by removing the side electrode of the plug—you would run into serious problems with cross-fire and arcing within the distributor cap.)

Now, from the point of view of the restorer or mechanic, it really doesn't matter what is going on electrically. We are not, after all, trying to design an ignition system. The only reason it is worth mentioning this is because of the effects the induced voltage has on the contact breaker that turns the current flow in the primary circuit on and off, and the extra step that has to be taken in order to protect those breaker points.

Because the electrical effects we are describing happen much faster than the mechanical action of the contact breaker, the points are only open a hair's breadth by the time the voltage surge in the primary occurs. Without some modification, this initially tiny air gap would be insufficient to block the jolt of energy in the primary circuit, and an arc would jump across the points, rapidly burning and pitting them (and also messing up what is happening to the secondary circuit). To prevent this—in effect to buy some time to allow the points to get fully open—a device called a capacitor or condenser is wired in parallel with the points.

The Condenser
A capacitor is a stunningly simple device. (For obscure reasons, this device is called a capacitor everywhere except in automotive applications, where it is universally known as a condenser.) It consists of two closely-spaced metal plates, separated by a thin insulator. In an automotive ignition condenser, the two metal "plates" are actually long strips of metal foil; the insulator is made of paper. This foil-paper-foil sandwich is then rolled up into a cylinder and stuffed into a small metal can. One of the foil strips is electrically connected to the case which, in turn, is attached to ground; the other is connected to a little "pigtail" of wire that extends out of the top of the can and is attached to the hot side of the contact points.

In action, the stream of surplus electrons that are threatening to jump the just-barely-open points takes, instead, the easier route into the conductive metal of one of the foil ribbons. By the time the condenser is full and no longer able to act as temporary storage for these electrons, the danger is past. When the points close again, the condenser conveniently discharges itself to ground.

Although it is a popular belief that the condensor also provides a bit of kick voltage that helps accelerate the collapse of the coil, this is not actually the case. The condensor and coil certainly form a resonant system, so there are moments during the event when the condensor adds a bit, but this effect is trivial. More to the point, it occurs long after the plug has begun to fire.

Ignition for Multi-Cylinder Engines
As it stands, this assembly of coil, breaker points, and condenser

> Although it is a popular belief that the condensor also provides a bit of kick voltage that helps accelerate the collapse of the coil, this is not actually the case. The condensor and coil certainly form a resonant system, so there are moments during the event when the condensor adds a bit, but this effect is trivial. More to the point, it occurs long after the plug has begun to fire.

will fire one spark plug, and is all a single-cylinder engine needs. (There are a few examples of "double-ended" coils, in which the "other" end of the secondary winding is routed to a second spark plug, rather than to a common connection with the hot side of the points. If the cam that operates the points is driven at crank speed, rather than half speed, this coil will fire two plugs at the same time, once every revolution of the crank. This will serve a two-cylinder engine, as it still does on the Harley-Davidson motorcycles of today. The extra spark per revolution occurs at the end of each cylinder's exhaust stroke, and though theoretically this should reduce spark plug life, it seems to do little harm.)

There have been a few multi-cylinder engines that use multiples of all these components, one set for each spark plug, but this, too, is rare. The near-universal arrangement is for the cam that trips the contact points to have a number of lobes equal to the number of cylinders, so a bolt of high voltage is created as many times per revolution of the cam as there are lobes—half that many per rotation of the crank. To feed the secondary voltage to the plugs, the business end of the secondary winding is routed to a high-tension distributor—a simple commutator, or rotary switch, that connects it to one plug after another, in sequence.

The sequencing is performed by a rotor that receives the juice through a carbon brush and sweeps around pointing at one terminal after another, each leading to one plug. In some early distributors, the rotor made actual physical contact with each terminal as it passed; this wore rapidly, however, and it was discovered that merely bringing the rotating tip close to the terminals worked just as well. The small air gap between the rotor tip and the terminal was insignificant, compared with the larger gap at the plug. For mechanical convenience, this high-tension distributor shares a common housing with the cam and breaker-points assembly.

Dual-Point Systems
The basic Kettering-type ignition system, as just described, was the standard wear for domestic passenger cars and trucks—and most others in the world—for 50 years, from the early 1920s

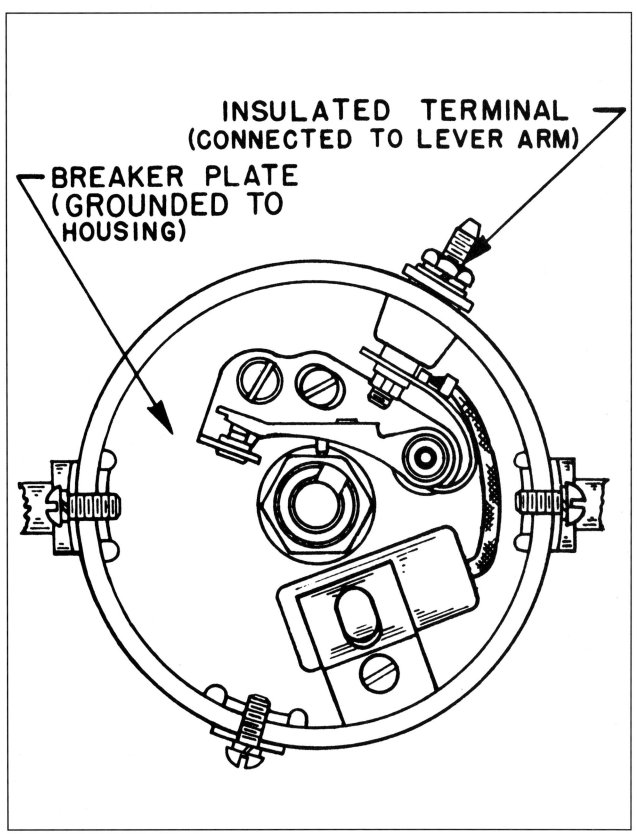

INSULATED TERMINAL
(CONNECTED TO LEVER ARM)

BREAKER PLATE
(GROUNDED TO
HOUSING)

The resemblance between this drawing and the following photograph is all the more amazing because the photo is of a Chevrolet distributor, while the line drawing is from a Ford. *Courtesy GM Canada*

through the early 1970s. About the only common variation, albeit a slight one, is found on Ford flathead V-8s, where there are two sets of points in the distributor. This was the first V-8 in really large-scale production and, in its day, it was a comparatively high-speed engine—the original 1932 engine gave peak horsepower at 3,400 rpm, which was as much as 1,000 rpm faster than other engines of that time. The combination of higher speed and more cylinders—a third more than a six, twice as many as a four—introduced the problem that, at high engine speeds, the coil was being called on to supply more sparks per minute than it could cope with.

To explain: Some time after each discharge of the coil, the points close again, which restores the flow of current through the primary circuit, and so re-establishes the magnetic field in the coil's core, ready for another interruption in the primary. The snag is that it takes a certain amount of time after the points close for the magnetic field to build to full strength—for the core to become "saturated." Although the required time is, in human terms, very short indeed, a 3,400 rpm V-8 demands more than 200 sparks per second, which does not provide even that brief interval. As a result, above a certain speed, the secondary voltage starts to dwindle, and a point is soon reached where the engine begins to misfire. Ford's solution was to recognize that the points are actually open far longer than necessary, with no current flowing in the primary winding during that time, so they provided two sets of points situated around the eight-lobed cam so that the second set re-established the circuit soon after the first set broke it.

Ballast Resistors
Actually, there is another component in the ignition system of most 12-volt cars of the pre-elec-

tronics era, and in some older 6-volt units, too, such as flathead Fords. This is the ignition resistor or ballast resistor.

It takes a fixed amount of time to saturate the core of the coil, and during that time the current flow through the coil is constantly increasing. Once saturation is reached, the coil's resistance is comparatively low, so rather a lot of current flows. This is why old cars that only potter about in parades can use up ignition points at a distressingly

---

If the engine is dead because there's no juice at the coil, though there is at the ignition switch, then a prime suspect is a ballast resistor that has burned out, leaving an open circuit. As a short-term emergency measure, you can "jump" around the resistor, connecting the wire feeding the resistor directly to the hot lead on the coil.

---

high rate. Because of the low engine speed, the coil spends a lot of time saturated, so its average resistance is low; because of the low resistance, a lot of current is passing through the points when they open, so the points burn out.

The designer's problem is to come up with a coil that has enough resistance (that is, enough turns of sufficiently fine wire) that it won't burn out either itself or the points, yet has *few enough* turns in the primary

winding to provide the necessary electrical output from the secondary winding at maximum engine speed. The whole problem would be a lot easier if only the resistance didn't vary so much. One way to reduce the variation in the draw of the coil is to place a fixed resistance in series with it. That way, the current that is flowing will vary according to the sum of the (varying) resistance of the coil and the (fixed) resistance of the ignition resistor. It still varies, but not as much as before.

If the engine is dead because there's no juice at the coil, though there is at the ignition switch, then a prime suspect is a ballast resistor that has burned out, leaving an open circuit. As a short-term emergency measure, you can "jump" around the resistor, connecting the wire feeding the resistor directly to the hot lead on the coil. This is a bad idea for the long term, however. If, for example, you're dealing with an engine swap, or someone else has done a "roll-your-own" job of installing or adapting a non-stock ignition system and the engine runs fine immediately after new points are installed, but you are cursed with points that seem to burn out frequently, the likely problem is a missing ballast resistor.

As noted, the coils for ballasted systems are designed differently from those for non-ballasted systems. This is the reason for the warning on some generic auto-supply-store coils that says, "use with external resistor." Beware: Coils supplied for specific models that are equipped with a ballast resistor may not have this warning, because the manufacturer expects the coil only to be used on that particular vehicle, and they know it has the resistor. If purchasing a coil intended for some other vehicle, ensure that you use a ballast resistor of the correct value if the source vehicle had one. Note also that some pre-electronic ignition Chevrolets, and many

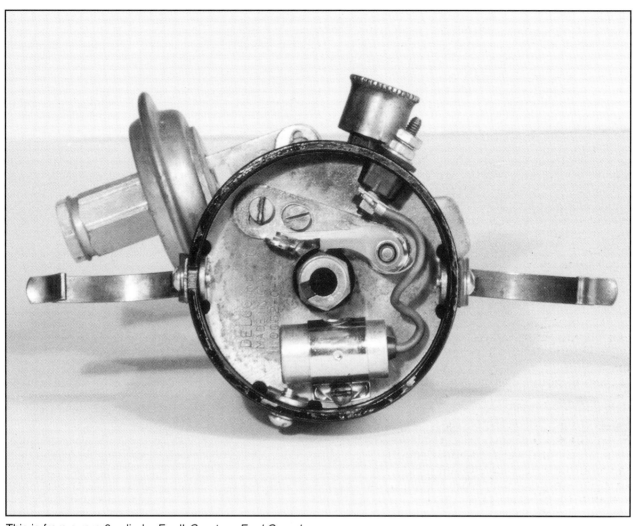

This is from a rare 6-cylinder Ford! *Courtesy Ford Canada*

other GM vehicles, use a length of stainless-steel resistance wire on the supply side of the coil, instead of a separate resistor. If ordinary hookup wire is used to replace this, an equivalent resistor has to be inserted in its place or the points will burn out rapidly and the coil will overheat.

Ballast-Resistor Bypass

Of course, any series resistance is going to reduce the primary voltage—in effect, the coil is operating at below battery voltage all the time. The Ford flathead ignition resistor, for example, drops the maximum voltage across the coil from a nominal 6 volts to about 4.5. This can obviously cre-

---

The limitations on high-speed performance of coil-and-breaker ignition encouraged race-engine builders to stick with magnetos.

---

ate its own problem when the battery voltage is low, particularly when starting.

Because of the huge draw of the starter, the battery voltage when cranking can drop to as lit-

tle as half the nominal system voltage, especially in cold weather. This robs the coil of primary voltage, so the secondary voltage might not be sufficient to jump the air gap in the spark plug, and the engine won't fire. (That's one reason why an engine might refuse to even cough when being cranked, even though it seems to be turning over fast enough, yet will burst to life with even the gentlest push start.)

Now, when a ballast resistor is used, we have a coil that is designed to produce an adequate secondary voltage output when the primary is running on reduced voltage—say, 7 or 8 volts in a 12-volt system. If we arrange

A "no-wires" contact breaker set from a Model A Ford. One contact screws into the condenser, which arrangement also provides the gap adjustment.

to feed the coil on full battery voltage when starting, the problem of voltage drop when starting is greatly eased. To prevent a potentially harmful excess current from eating the coil and the points, we then arrange to switch the resistor back into the circuit once the engine is running.

When running normally, the supply to the hot lead of the coil passes through the ballast resistor; for starting, the resistor is switched out of the circuit. The usual arrangement to bypass the resistor is to provide an extra terminal at the starter solenoid which is live only when the starter is energized, and to run a wire from that terminal to the coil; 12-volt Chrysler products bypass the resistor at the ignition

Because of the huge draw of the starter, the battery voltage when cranking can drop to as little as half the nominal system voltage, especially in cold weather. This robs the coil of primary voltage, so the secondary voltage might not be sufficient to jump the air gap in the spark plug, and the engine won't fire.

switch. Flathead Fords that have a starter relay fitted but retain 6-volt ignition (and any other rarities that use an ignition resistor in a 6-volt system) can benefit from the installation of such a bypass.

Advantages of Electronic Ignition

The limitations on high-speed performance of coil-and-breaker ignition encouraged race-engine builders to stick with magnetos, the output of which actually increases with speed, and the poor low-speed behavior of which was unimportant in that application. For that latter reason, though, magnetos were generally unsatisfactory for passenger cars, and in such applications the Ket-

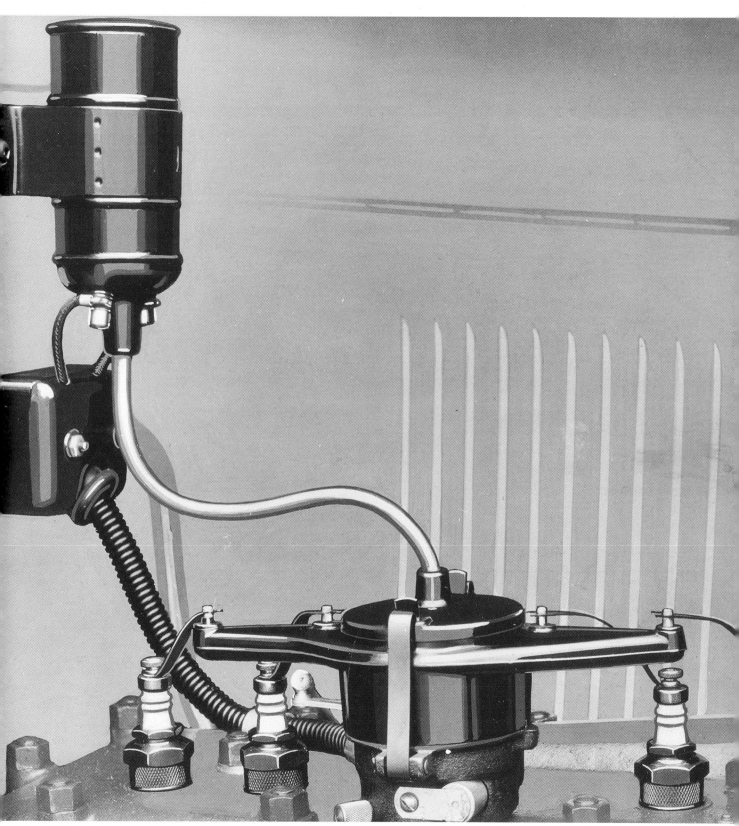

While the lower part of most distributors contains the contact breakers, the upper part holds the rotor that distributes the output of the coil to each cylinder in sequence. The "wings" on the distributor cap on this 1930 Model A Ford minimize the length of the high-tension leads. Note the uninsulated high-tension leads. *Courtesy Ford Canada*

tering system, given regular maintenance, works adequately well—though only just. At the very least, it is certainly an advance on hot-tube ignition! The major catch is the need for regular maintenance, but there are other drawbacks as well.

One of the weak spots of the coil-and-breaker system is the breaker points, especially the fiber rubbing block on the moveable half of the point set that contacts the rotating cam. As this wears down, the point gap gradually closes. Eventually, it would diminish to zero, at which point the engine would stop. Before that, though, the same wear causes the rubbing block to contact the cam ever closer to the peak of the lobe, so the points open progressively later, and the ignition timing gets more and more retarded. The second limitation of the coil-and-breaker system is the current-switching capacity of the points. Despite the presence of the condenser, a primary current of more than five or six amps will tend to cause burning and arcing at the points, shortening their life. This, in turn, places a restriction on the strength of the magnetic field that can be stored in the coil, which limits the amount of power available to fire the plug. Third, at very high engine speeds, the points tend to "bounce"—the moveable half of the points can no longer faithfully follow the contour of the distributor cam.

Finally, there is the business of "dwell." With a cam-and-breaker arrangement, the primary has current flowing through it for a certain fixed number of degrees of engine rotation, but the length of *time* that the current is flowing varies with engine speed. This leads to an ugly choice. On the one hand, if you keep the dwell angle small, the coil will have insufficient time to become fully saturated at high engine speeds, leading to a high-speed miss. On the other hand, if you arrange for a longer

dwell time—say by using a distributor cam with a different lobe shape, so the points spend more time closed and less time open, or through something like the Ford flathead's dual-point system—then at low speeds the primary becomes saturated early in the cycle, but then the current keeps flowing because the points are still closed, so the coil will tend to overheat.

These first began to emerge as serious problems during the 1960s, when manufacturers were heavily engaged in a horsepower race; compression ratios as high as 12:1, combined with engine

---

One of the weak spots of the coil-and-breaker system is the breaker points, especially the fiber rubbing block on the moveable half of the point set. As this wears down, the point gap gradually closes.

---

speeds over 6,000 rpm, tested the upper limits of coil-and-breaker ignition, and it became clear that the days of the classic Kettering system were numbered. Ironically, what finally ensured the emergence and universal adoption of modern electronic ignition was not street hemis or other monster motors, but rather the introduction of emissions legislation in the 1970s. Though compression ratios tumbled and revs abated, the need to fire very lean mixtures, and to do so reliably throughout the life of the car, became the new factors that finally eliminated contact points. When you're scraping to meet

standards for the emission of hydrocarbons—essentially unburned fuel—you can't afford even one misfire in ten thousand, and when you have to certify the engine's emissions for 50,000 miles without a tune-up, you need a system that doesn't depend on breaker points that constantly wear, retarding the timing, and that can still fire a spark plug when its gap has eroded open to 0.050 inch or more.

The solution that was eventually adopted (we're skipping over a brief flirtation with capacitor discharge systems in the early 1970s) retained the familiar induction coil, but eliminated the problems of contact points by eliminating the points themselves. Instead of a mechanical switch to turn on and off the current flow in the primary windings of the coil, the switching is done electronically. In the place where you would expect to find the distributor cam sits a rotating magnet, with a number of "teeth" or poles corresponding to the number of cylinders. As each protruding pole of that rotating magnet passes a fixed pickup head, a small pulse of electricity is produced. That pulse is then used to trigger a transistor—an electronic relay—that briefly interrupts, then quickly restores, the current in the primary winding of the coil.

There are two major advantages to this scheme compared to a conventional points-and-condenser system, plus a third minor one that doesn't really apply to most older cars. First, the constant wear on the rubbing block is eliminated, so timing remains accurate and no adjustment or replacement is ever needed. Second, when you remove the concern over the amount of juice you can put through a pair of small, exposed metallic contact points, the current in the primary circuit can be dramatically increased, so the coil can be redesigned to provide a greater secondary voltage

A Ford dual-point distributor from 1935. Note also the dual rotors used with separate distributor caps for the left and right banks of cylinders. *Courtesy Ford Canada*

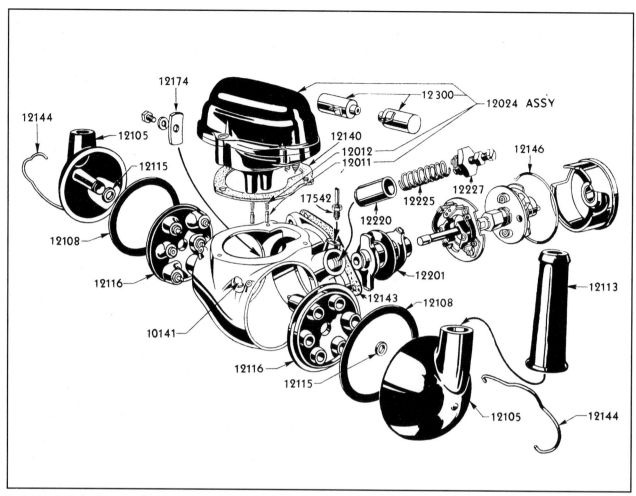

An integrated distributor and dual coil assembly from a 12-cylinder Lincoln Zephyr. *Courtesy Ford Canada*

output that can fire a plug with a gap that is larger, whether by design or as a result of wear, without the risk of frying the points. As long as there is enough juice to jump the gap, a wider plug gap provides a bigger spark, and that means it's more likely to light the mixture in the cylinder. (Contrary to some opinion, the actual amount of energy in the spark *does* matter; the old belief that "the mixture doesn't care if it's lit by a match or by a blowtorch" is just plumb mistaken.) The same increase in potential output from the coil also means you can fire a plug that has some additional insulation, beyond the air gap, between its electrodes, such as one that is soaked in gasoline.

> Ironically, what finally ensured the emergence and universal adoption of modern electronic ignition was not street hemis or other monster motors, but rather the introduction of emissions legislation.

The electronics inside the "black box" that forms the brains of an electronic ignition system makes this possible because it can, in effect, vary the dwell angle. At low engine speeds, a timing circuit inside the electronics box delays restoring the primary current until it judges there is just enough time remaining to saturate the core. At higher speeds, it tries to keep the dwell time nearly constant, allowing primary current to flow during a larger number of crank degrees. This feature, together with freedom from the current limitations of breaker points, is what permits the redesign of the coil to give potentially more secondary output, without cooking the coil through an excessive primary current.

Finally, with no mechanical movement at the points, there is no problem with point bounce. For low-revving older motors, though, this never was an issue and never will be.

Now, muscle cars are certainly a legitimate part of the collectible car scene, and they can surely benefit from an updated ignition system, but some of the same factors that eventually drove Detroit to abandon points-and-condenser ignition can be a significant factor for other, less brawny collectible vehicles. For example, even when they're in "like-new" shape, older engines may tend to draw more oil into the combustion chamber past piston rings and valve-guide seals, and that oil tends to foul the spark plugs. Also, early carburetor and manifold designs, especially on inline engines, often have poor mixture distribution patterns—some cylinders will run lean, others too rich. The potentially higher voltage output of a modern electronically-switched coil will light the fire in such an engine when a points-type system wouldn't.

Electronic Ignition Conversions

Happily, in many cases there is a modern breaker-less distributor that will drop directly into the hole the old "flintlock" distributor came out of. For most others, conversion kits are available to adapt high-tech innards into the original distributor housing. The replacement parts comprise a magnet wheel to replace the cam; a mounting plate that replaces the original one that the points were attached to, and onto which the fixed pickup head is fastened;

the pickup head itself; the electronics box that contains the switching transistor, the dwell time regulation, and a bunch of other electronics (don't ask!); a new coil; plus a few odds and ends of hardware.

In some cases, the rotating magnet just slips in place of the distributor cam; in others this conversion involves turning down the original distributor cam on a lathe, reducing it to a simple cylindrical slug of metal, to form a hub onto which the magnet wheel supplied in the kit is pressed. You

---

Apart from the advantages for cold-weather starting and the ability to cope with fouled or worn plugs, why not put in something you won't ever have to change again, as long as you're putting in new parts?

---

might suppose in this case that the "phasing" of the magnet wheel is a problem—that you would have to arrange for the protruding spokes to be lined up in exactly the same place as the peaks of the lobe on the original cam. That's not so. First, note that on an eight-cylinder engine, there would have been eight lobes on the cam, or one every 45

degrees. The furthest out the placement of the magnet wheel could be, then, is half that much—22.5 degrees—and there is a sufficient range of adjustment in the rotational position of the plate that holds the pickup head to allow the plate to be swiveled around so the pickup is in the right relationship relative to one spoke—any spoke—on the magnet wheel.

Apart from the advantages for cold-weather starting and the ability to cope with fouled or worn plugs, why not put in something you won't ever have to change again, as long as you're putting in new parts? Other than occasional spark plug replacement, a modern breaker-less ignition system should require no attention at all for decades.

A final point worth noting here is that coils actually appear to "age," even when stored from new. Despite the fact that they consist simply of two windings of copper wire around a central core of iron and have no moving parts, their performance falls off as years go by, so the output of an NOS (new old stock) coil is likely to be lower than it was when it was first manufactured. The problem may lie with the shellac insulation applied to the copper wire before winding that prevents adjacent turns of wire from shorting together, effectively reducing the number of turns. Whatever the cause, carefully instrumented tests have confirmed the effect. This is another solid argument for upgrading older ignition systems.

Lights

6

One of the factors that makes modern cars safer than those of earlier years is bright lights—bright head lamps to see with, and bright tail, stop, and turn lights to help others see you. A serious shortcoming on a lot of older cars is feeble lighting equipment, and though you may not plan on doing a lot of driving after dark, there may be times when you will have no choice about the matter. Consider, too, that brake lights (and maybe just one of them!) that give off little more light than the glow of a cigarette is an invitation to get tail-ended, even during daylight hours—perhaps especially then. Also, the police may not be sympathetic to the foibles of ancient machinery; even if your lighting system is working like new, you may get cited for a safety violation if like new isn't good enough. Inclement weather makes things doubly worse. It is no fun whatsoever to be caught in rain at night, peering through a misty slot in a windshield swept by slow, deficient wipers, into the gloom cast by a pair of funky headlights, while traffic from behind closes at perhaps 40 miles per hour. There are some solutions; we'll start with headlights first.

Headlights

Prior to World War II, headlights came in a huge assortment of sizes and shapes, but the general arrangement was a replaceable bulb with two filaments, which latched into a socket with a bayonet fitting within a separate reflector of silvered glass. Each filament provided 32 candlepower and drew about 4 amps; the only difference between high and low beam was the aim and focus of the bulb filament. A molded-glass lens with some sort of prism pattern covered the front, though sometimes the reflector and lens were made in one piece, with the bulb fitting in from the back.

When new, these units gave a marginally satisfactory light, but the impossibility of sealing the silvered surface of the

---

Sealed-beam conversion kits are available for most pre-1940 cars from a number of specialist suppliers, some of which are noted in the Appendix. If you don't insist on retaining absolutely original appearance, this conversion makes it easy to provide yourself with decent headlights.

---

reflector against the ravages of weather meant that the reflector rapidly tarnished and grew dull—half the light output could be lost in a matter of months. Also, the multi-piece assembly meant that wear and production variances could leave the bulb filament slightly misaligned with respect to the reflector; some very early models (pre-1934) even required that the position of the

bulb be adjusted to bring it into the correct focus.

All this changed effective with the 1940 model year with the introduction of sealed-beam lights that completely eliminated the problem of reflector darkening and "misfocused" bulbs by enclosing both the precisely aligned bulb filament and the silvered surface inside a one-piece glass envelope. The use of sealed beams soon became mandatory on all new cars, and apart from a slight increase in the output of the high-beam filament, this standardized design remained unchanged until the industry changeover to 12-volt lighting in the middle 1950s.

Sealed-beam conversion kits are available for most pre-1940 cars from a number of specialist suppliers, some of which are noted in the appendix. If you don't insist on retaining absolutely original appearance, this conversion makes it easy to provide yourself with decent headlights; even if you're retaining a 6-volt system, sealed-beams for that voltage are still available, though a bit scarce now. There are a couple of cautions, though. First, you will be hard pressed to find a conversion kit for a car with headlight housings that have some odd, non-round shape. Second, the increase in wattage from the original 32/32-watt bulbs to the 35/45- or 40/50-watt filaments in the sealed-beams will mean a corresponding increase in current through switches and wiring. In chapter seven, we strongly recommended the use of a headlight relay as a means of milking the best possible performance out of a six-volt system; if heftier headlights are installed, this move should be regarded as vital rather than optional.

If you are unwilling to accept the non-authentic appearance of a sealed-beam conversion, a significant improvement in light output is still possible, though it will prove rather more difficult and expensive to achieve. Just as with getting top performance out of a starter, it is vitally important to keep the voltage drop between the battery post and the headlight filament as low as possible—a 10 percent drop in voltage will cost about one third in light output, no matter whether the system is running on 6 volts or 12. Again, the first step should be fitting a relay. While headlight relays for 12-volt systems are commonplace, 6-volt units are rare. It seems there are

no domestic manufacturers of these items, though the German firm Bosch still lists one 6-volt relay suitable for headlight applications; the part number is 0332 204 001. Alternatively, you might consider adapting a suitable industrial (non-automotive) relay. The points to bear in mind are that the relay's coil should be

> If you are unwilling to accept the non-authentic appearance of a sealed-beam conversion, a significant improvement in light output is still possible.

rated at 6 volts, or close to it, that the contacts will handle the current draw on high beam, and that the unit is sufficiently rugged to resist vibration and is sealed against moisture and dirt. One unit that seems to meet these criteria is the Aromat model CA, as listed in the appendix. In addition, careful attention must be paid to the quality of the electrical connections, both on the supply and the ground side.

The next point to attend to is the state of the reflector. If the silvering is simply darkened, "sloshing" it with one of the clear liquid silver cleaners will achieve a significant improvement. Beware, though, of conventional silver polishes that are applied as a thick milky fluid, allowed to dry, and then polished off—the silvering on headlight reflectors

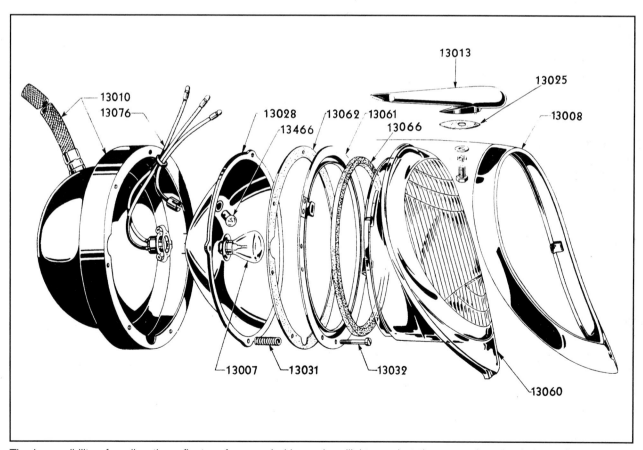

The impossibility of sealing the reflector of pre-sealed-beam headlights against the atmosphere is obvious. *Courtesy Ford Canada*

is so thin that the abrasive in this type of polish will scour right through it to bare metal! If the reflectors are seriously deteriorated, they will need to be refinished. A number of companies offer a re-silvering service, but without a hermetic seal the tarnishing will immediately begin again. One option is chrome plating, but this is hardly satisfacto-ry—while it will not tarnish, chromium is only about two thirds as shiny as silver. The Uvira company offers a refinishing process that involves a vacuum deposited layer of aluminum inside the refinished shell, protected by a thin transparent coating. The results are claimed to be within a couple of percent of new silver, and the brightness is guar-anteed to last. Of course, before any re-plating or refinishing operation, any dents or distortion of the shape of the reflectors must be attended to.

If you have installed a relay, you can take advantage of replacement bulbs with 50-watt high-beam filaments to fit inside your new reflectors. Halogen bulbs of even greater output are

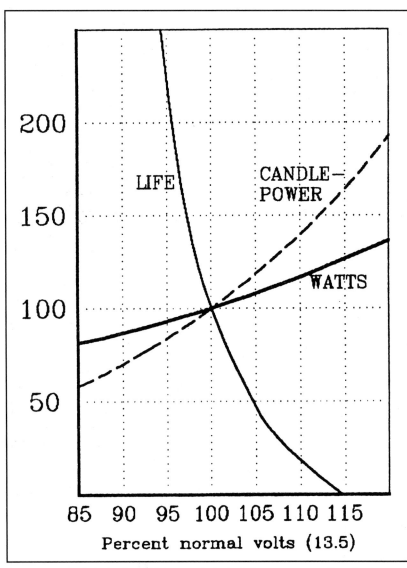

As more power is fed to it, the light output of a bulb increases more than the increase in power, though the life of the bulb drops even faster. Note that just a 10 percent drop in voltage cuts light output by more than one third.

> The lights at the rear of many older vehicles provided barely enough notice to other drivers when they were new; with rusted reflectors and massive voltage drops from funky wiring and connections, they are completely inadequate.

also available, together with adapters to make the sockets match. Beware: The added heat may introduce the risk of cracking the lens, and the extra current draw demands tip-top wiring and grounds.

Taillamps
Being seen is arguably as important as seeing. The lights at the rear of many older vehicles provided barely enough notice to other drivers when they were new; with rusted reflectors and massive voltage drops from funky wiring and connections, they are completely inadequate.

First, the voltage drops. The problems of excessive resistance in both the supply wiring and the grounds are potentially worse at the back end of a car than at the front, not only because of the extra distance from the bulb to the battery but also because of the increased probability of corrosion having done its dirty work on the ground connections. As elsewhere, the first order of business is to minimize the total resistance of the circuit by ensuring adequate wire gauges, clean connections that are protected against the intrusion of water, and to pay close attention to the hidden half of the wiring—the return path from the component to the battery ground post. This would be a good time to review chapter nine. As noted there, a reasonably bulletproof method of ensuring a secure ground connection is to run a ground bus—an extra wire running from the ground side of all the rear lights directly back to the battery ground post, or as close to it (electrically) as practicality and concerns about original appearance permit. Remember, this added wire has to carry all the current that might be supplied at one time to all of the lamps it serves.

A small halogen bulb in the brake-light socket will get the attention of following traffic.

Assuming that the purely electrical considerations are taken care of, the next problem is the nature of the reflectors for the rear light(s). In many cases, the only reflector was a layer of silver or white paint inside the lamp housing. With time, this paint flakes off, leaving a reflector that consists simply of rust. Re-painting the interior of the lamp housing will restore original appearance; it will not help much with the visibility problem. As with headlight shells, it may be worthwhile to have them silvered or chrome plated, though again note that the silvering will rapidly darken unless an absolutely airtight seal can be achieved. An alternative is to have the entire housing cadmium plated—both inside and out, which saves having to mask the exterior. Cadmium on the outside makes a good paint base and, while cadmium is only a small fraction as reflective as silver or even chrome, on the inside it is a good deal better than paint. Another "quick-and-dirty" fix is to line the housing with aluminum foil, shiny side out, though this too will quickly become dull, to say nothing of the inevitable crinkles.

Though there is reason to be cautious about halogen headlights in old cars, halogen taillamps are a different matter. Bosch make a series of low-powered halogen bulbs with a base that fits a single-contact bayonet socket. Part number 64113 specifies a 10-watt unit; number 64115 is a 20-watt item. Both these are 12-volt bulbs; alas, there seems to be no 6-volt equivalent. Depending on the application, they may just plug right in. (Caution: Don't handle the outside of a halogen bulb with your bare hands—the fingerprint can cause local overheating and cracking of the glass bulb.) Even if a direct plug-in replacement is not possible, it is no particular challenge for anyone that can operate a drill and a pop-rivet gun to modify the original tail-lamp bracket to take an appropriate socket. If even this seems like too much work, or if you want to provide separate bulbs for tail and brake lights, there are aftermarket replacement brackets available for many early Fords and Chevs that provide *two* single-contact sockets. A small halogen bulb in the brake-light socket will get the attention of following traffic.

Living With Six Volts

7

If it is your aim to rebuild to an absolutely factory-original condition that would pass the most rigorous, nit-picking inspection, then you are stuck with whatever kind of electrical system the car was initially manufactured with, and for most vehicles built between the end of World War I and the middle 1950s that means a system that runs on 6 volts. All you can hope to do, in this case, is to get that 6-volt system back to the same shape it was in when it left the factory. Since you are aiming at true authenticity, you won't be up-rating components for either performance or convenience, and you certainly won't be adding such modern accessories as tape players or power windows, so a like-new 6-volt system should serve as well as it did when new, which is to say adequately well under favorable circumstances.

There are a couple of problems, though. First is the issue of "like new." As cars age, corrosion takes an increasing toll, affecting not just the appearance of the body panels and the strength of the mechanical parts, but also the integrity of the connections within the various electrical circuits. Over the years, ground straps rot away, crusty greenish-white growths develop around terminals, fuse holders rust, and glaze builds up on the surface of generator and motor commutators.

Now, a slightly corroded bulb socket or switch contact or battery terminal may not contribute substantial resistance by itself, but because the juice has to pass through several of these deteriorated connections, the total resistance can drop the system voltage by 1.5 to 2 volts, or more. That's between a quarter and a third of what's available with a 6-volt system, which saps starter performance, makes lights burn dimly, slows down the wipers, and generally squelches system performance.

Restoration of the electrics of an old car to like-new condition, then, means painstaking reconditioning of each and every electrical connection in the system. What's more, no sooner is the job done than the corrosion starts all over again (rust never sleeps!), so a certain amount of

---

Restoration of the electrics of an old car to like-new condition means painstaking reconditioning of each and every electrical connection in the system.

---

on-going maintenance is necessary to stay ahead of the effects of continued aging. (And if you demand an absolutely "pure" restoration, you even exclude the possibility of battling the rot by covering exposed terminals with boots, heat-shrink tubing, or other non-original parts.)

The second problem is the matter of "favorable circumstances." Remember that it was not until comparatively recently that people took for granted that a car could be operated all year round. For one thing, ethylene glycol antifreeze did not completely replace the earlier methyl-alcohol-based antifreezes until the 1950s; also, really effective heaters and defrosters were rare before that time. Since it is damn near impossible to get an engine with a 6-volt electrical system to start at 40 below, it is probably no mere coincidence that domestic manufacturers switched from 6- to 12-volt systems about the same time, in 1955–1956.

"Favorable circumstances," then, means moderate weather, among other things. This may not be much of a problem if you live in California, but you can pretty much forget about winter driving with a 6-volt car in the northern parts of North America. On the other hand, when there's snow on the ground in those areas, there is also likely to be salt and sand around, too, and anyone locked into a "cherry" restoration is unlikely to submit their pride and joy to a bath in brine.

It is not hard to understand why manufacturers changed from 6 volts to 12 in the middle 1950s, what's puzzling is why they ever had 6-volt systems to start with! Inquiries to several auto and battery manufacturers and other expert sources has failed to turn up a consistent answer to this question. Here are some of the various explanations that have been offered:

1. The first widespread application of storage batteries to automobiles was the 6-volt "Hotshot" dry-cell battery used to energize the trembler-coil ignition system on some model T Fords; everyone else just went along.

2. Before the advent of modern case materials, the size and weight of a 12-volt battery was about twice that of a 6-volt unit. It just didn't seem practical to install such a bulky, hefty item.

3. A 12-volt battery uses more lead than a 6-volt unit, but permits lighter wiring; the choice between the two may have depended on the relative costs of copper versus lead at various times in history.

And we have our own speculation about why the change occurred when it did, rather than earlier or later—see the sidebar A Zany Theory.

Battery

If, despite the drawbacks, you should decide to stick with a 6-volt

---

It is not hard to understand why manufacturers changed from 6 volts to 12 in the middle 1950s, what's puzzling is why they ever had 6-volt systems to start with!

---

system, then you are going to need all the help you can get. First, you should seek out a 6-volt battery with the highest CCA rating (see chapter two) you can find that will fit. That in itself may conflict with original appearance, which is probably the most common reason for retaining a 6-volt system in the first place! This conflict arises because much of the advance in battery performance over the past 30 or 40 years can be attributed to the introduction of new materials for cases, which allows them to be made thinner than the hard rubber cases and "tar-tops" of earlier days, leaving

The first order of business in getting reliable operation from a 6-volt system is getting the heftiest 6-volt battery you can find. The Optima battery looks odd, but the 6-volt unit pictured at bottom right delivers a thumping 850 cold cranking amps. *Courtesy Optima Batteries, Inc.*

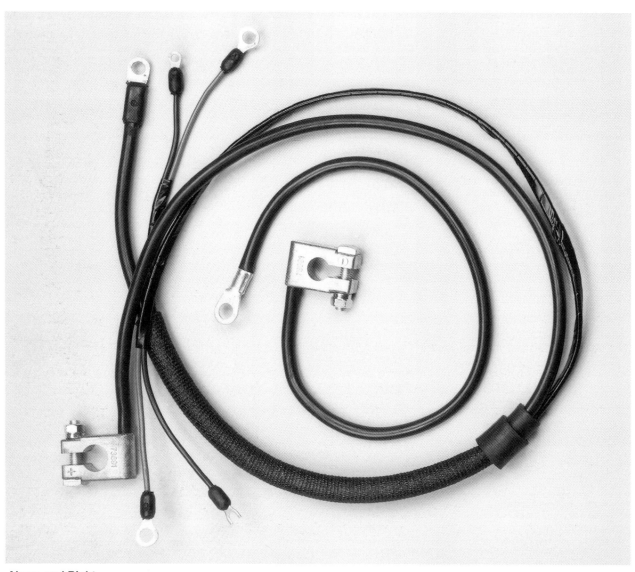

Above and Right
Equally important is ensuring short, direct grounds, using fat cables with professionally secured terminals. *Courtesy Antique Auto Battery Manufacturing Co.*

more room inside for lead plates and acid. New materials allow thinner separators, too, which again increases the volume available for the working parts. Batteries of original appearance, on the other hand, generally use near-original construction methods and materials.

Of course, if your car's battery was originally located somewhere out of sight, under the seat, for example, this may not be a problem. If the battery lives somewhere visible, though, about

> First, you should seek out a 6-volt battery with the highest CCA rating you can find that will fit.

all you can do is fit a powerful modern battery for daily operation, then switch back to a tar-top when you want to present an authentic appearance. If this

should be your approach, then for ease in switching back and forth the two batteries should at least have terminals that are similar both in size and in location.

Starter Cables and Direct Grounds
Since the reason for searching for a battery with a hefty CCA rating is to get the highest possible voltage across the terminals when a very large current is briefly flowing, it is equally important to reduce to a minimum any voltage

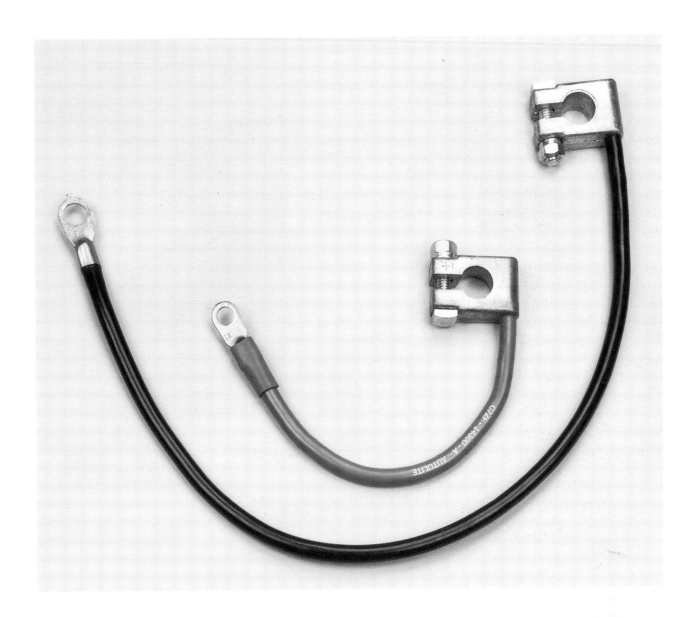

drop between the battery and the starter. As already noted, you want big fat cables with clean, low resistance terminals to minimize voltage drops, but factory-original battery cables are usually as small as the manufacturer thinks he can get away with. In 6-volt systems, the stock cable from the battery to the starter solenoid was usually no larger than #02 gauge (0.4575-inch conductor outside diameter), and often as slim as #2 gauge (0.330-inch conductor outside diameter). Electrical cable of #02 gauge and larger is available from a surprising source—your nearest arc-welders' supply outfit!

Not only can you purchase cable of truly substantial size there, it will also be made up of many more strands than a typical automotive battery cable of the same gauge, and the added flexibility may ease routing.

Suitable cable terminals are available from various mail-order sources, and the same outfit that sells the cable may be able to secure your terminals to the cable they supply; otherwise, you're shopping for a gigantic pair of crimping pliers. Remember, as with ordinary hookup wire, but to an even greater extent, it is important that the cable should

completely fill the hole in the terminal once it is crimped. Filling gaps with solder just isn't satisfactory. On no account use bolt-on battery terminals; while they will serve for an emergency repair, these tend to have high resistance even when new, and corrosion will rapidly increase that resistance.

The cables running from the battery's hot terminal to the starter relay, and from there to the starter, are just one half of the circuit; the other half—the ground—needs equal attention. While some modern vehicles are conspicuously slipshod in this regard (there is one popular model that seems to depend entirely on the throttle, clutch, and shift linkage to complete the path from the engine to ground!), earlier vehicles, too, are often victims of excessive resistance in the path from the starter back to ground, even when everything is in like-new condition. In almost all cases, the starter is indirectly grounded by being bolted to the engine block, which is itself indirectly grounded by an un-insulated strap running to the chassis, with a third cable connecting the chassis to the ground terminal on the battery.

It takes very little thought to realize that, apart from there

---

You want big fat cables with clean, low resistance terminals, to minimize voltage drops, but factory-original battery cables are usually as small as the manufacturer thinks he can get away with.

---

being too many connections, they have arranged things the wrong way round! If the object is to reduce the voltage drop—rather than to cut to the absolute minimum the amount of copper wire you have to buy—then the electrical return path should run from the starter case directly to the battery ground terminal, letting the indirect ground (via the connection between the starter and the block) handle the comparatively small load of the ignition system.

You can arrange this for yourself by running a ground cable directly between the battery ground terminal and one of the

mounting bolts for the starter. This should be of the same gauge that feeds from the battery hot lead to the starter, via the starter switch or relay. Again, authentic original appearance will be compromised, though it may be possible to make the non-original connections unobtrusive, if not invisible. Of course, to provide a ground for everything else on the car, the battery ground has to be connected to the chassis, but the original ground strap connecting the engine to the chassis takes care of this.

As to the starter itself, at the very least it must be in as-new condition, matching the original factory specs for stall torque and no-load rpm. Any local starter/generator shop will be able to check your existing starter on these criteria, and to turn down a scored commutator and/or fit new brushes and bearings (see also chapter three). They may also be able to re-wind your existing starter field coils with a smaller number of turns of heavier-gauge wire so that the starter draws more current and so develops more torque. If not, some of the specialist firms that serve the collectible-car fraternity offer this service, or sell such high-torque starters, either outright or on exchange.

Charging

Then there is the problem of keeping your brute 6-volt battery charged. The rated output, in amperes, of the generator originally fitted to your car will usually be stamped onto the case, noted on a tag on the generator, or can be found among the specifications in the workshop or owner's manuals. Note that this figure is the generator's maximum output at its maximum rpm when in new condition; generator output will drop with age, as a glaze forms on the surface of the commutator and as brush wear allows the springs that hold them in contact with the commutator to relax somewhat. Worn bearings or bushings will also affect output, as excessive radial free play randomly affects the clearance between the armature and the field coils. A generator's output also drops as the temperature climbs—the ratings are basically for a room-temperature test. And since the generator's output is a function of how fast it is spinning, at highway cruising speeds you shouldn't count on more than about three quarters of maximum.

To give yourself a wider margin of comfort, you might try to find a higher-output generator from a different model of the same car, or a larger make/model from the same manufacturer. With luck, you may even find one having the same dimensions and external appearance as the original, requiring only a deft swapping of the identifying tag to hoodwink the concours judges and other nit-pickers. If all else fails, specialist electrical suppliers to car collectors may be able to re-wind your original generator for greater output.

Whatever you might do in this regard, though, recall from chapter three that generators do not develop any useful output until they are spinning at a good clip; there's likely no generator that will fit that can provide enough "oomph" to achieve a charge when the engine is idling. Alternators, however, have the ability to produce a useful amount of juice at the lowest speed the motor is likely to run; that's why they have completely replaced the DC generator in automotive applications. But a 6-volt alternator? You bet!

Remember the diodes in the alternator that invert the "wrong-way" portion of the alternator's internal AC? With a little internal re-wiring, that diode characteristic can be used to block half of the alternator's out-

put, yielding 6 volts. Unfortunately, done just as described, the current is cut in half too, so a 50-amp, 12-volt alternator converted in this way will put out just 25 amps of 6-volt current.

This kind of conversion is very much the province of specialists, however. It's not so much that the actual theory is that tough to grasp, it's that the tools needed to dismantle the alternator, press out diodes, etc., cost more than a completely reworked unit from one of those

specialist firms. These same folks can often also supply appropriate brackets, and pulleys in widths to suit your fan belt. There *are* some authentic, purpose-built 6-volt alternators that do not suffer from the problem of the current output being halved. Check the specs carefully before you give anyone your credit-card number—at a minimum, you want something with at least the same rated amperage as the original generator, and preferably a little more. At the same time,

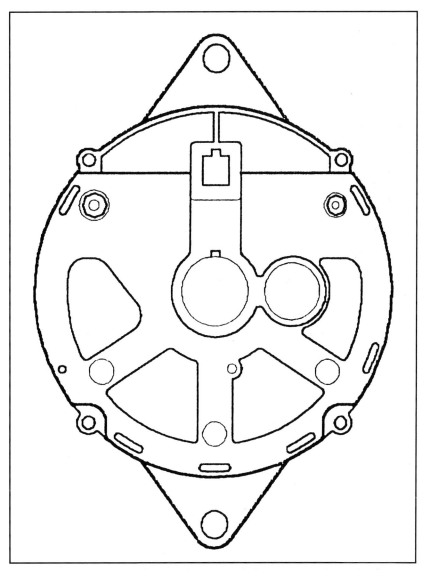

The first-generation Delco alternator is comparatively easy to convert to 6-volt operation—all you need is a suitable 6-volt regulator. This unit can also be swapped from negative- to positive-ground operation, though this is a specialist operation.

this is not a case of "if some is good, more is better"—it is unwise to fit an alternator that could potentially result in a melt down if the regulator should fail and allow the full output of a monster alternator to flow to your battery. In most cases, these alternators have internal regulators, so there's no new regulator to install.

Of course, there's no way you can disguise an alternator, so this kind of conversion immediately trashes any hope of maintaining authentic original appearance, though with a bit of planning it ought to be possible to arrange the mounting brackets to permit swapping back to the authentic generator for when you want to present an authentic original appearance.

Headlight Relays

For a given quality of reflector, the only way to get more light out is to put more electricity in. With low-powered bulb-type headlights, the electrical demand is sufficiently modest that it is practical to run all of the juice that feeds the headlights through the headlight and dimmer switches— the cheapest and most convenient routing.

As headlights were made brighter, though, their electrical demands increased until the point was reached that the wiring and the contacts in the switch contributed enough resistance to limit headlight performance and to generate a noticeable amount of heat. (Grasp an old headlight

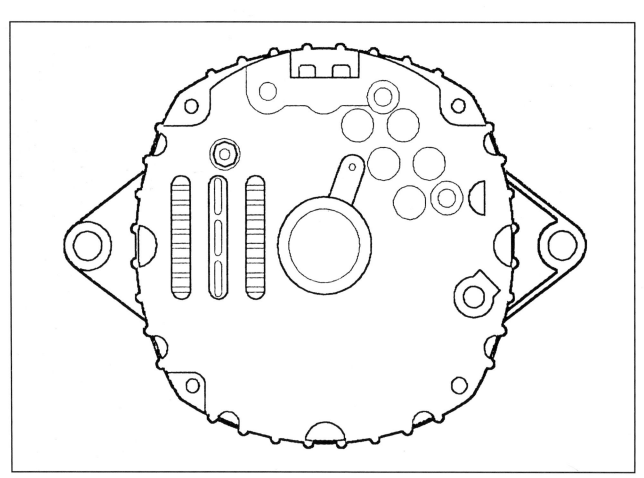

This diagram shows the second-generation Delco alternator.

switch that's been feeding a pair of high beams for a while—they get warm, sometimes very warm!)

Though only a few manufacturers had bothered with them before, most cars built after the introduction of sealed-beams in 1940 were fitted with headlight relays, which reduced the voltage drop between battery and lights

> To give yourself a wider margin of comfort, you might try to find a higher-output generator from a different model of the same car. With luck, you may even find one having the same dimensions and external appearance as the original.

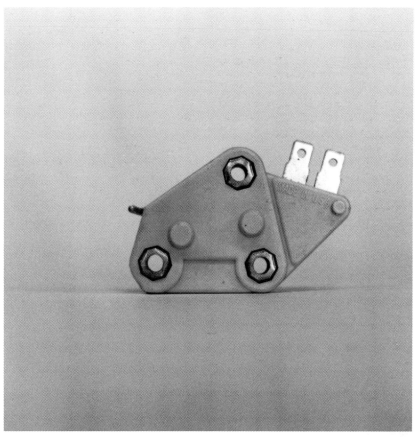

The later, second-generation Delco alternator can also be converted for 6-volt, negative-ground operation by the replacement of its 12-volt regulator with this 6-volt unit.

by reducing the length of the wire run and by providing a heftier set of contacts than could conveniently be crammed into a dash switch. For owners of the "orphans" that still were not so equipped, aftermarket headlight relays were sold as an add-on accessory.

As explained in chapter four, a relay is simply an electromagnet coil that, when energized, closes a set of contacts. When applied to headlights, the headlight switch only has to carry the current needed to activate the relay coil. With the relay located close to the headlights, the wiring run is much reduced, which directly improves lamp performance, as does the fact that a clean, large set of internal contacts carries the current, rather than an old, oxidized small set of contacts in the headlight switch. The reduced electrical load on the switch will greatly extend its life, too. If appearance considerations force you to locate the relay somewhere remote from the lights, at least try to keep the wiring run as short as possible, and in every case use fat wires—at least #10 gauge.

Six-volt relays have become quite rare. Apart from used and NOS ones available at swap meets, there is at least one automotive relay that is appropriate, and an industrial item that *might* be suitable. These are noted in chapter six. All 6-volt cars could use headlight relays; if the vehicle has been upgraded from bulb-type to sealed-beam headlights, they should be regarded as essential.

Changing from Six Volts to Twelve

8

Whatever you might do with a 6-volt system to minimize its shortcomings, the fact remains that any resistance in a 6-volt system causes twice the voltage drop as the same resistance in a 12-volt system. Twelve volts, in short, are better than 6. The usual reasons, then, for upgrading from 6 to 12 volts are greater reliability, reduced electrical-system maintenance, and the opportunity to add modern electrical accessories. Happily, such a conversion is usually quite practical, and less of a wholesale parts swap than you might think.

It is power that makes things go, and power (in watts) is volts times amps, so if you double the voltage you get the same power at just half the amperage. Wiring and contacts, on the other hand, are rated in *amps*, so 6-volt wiring, connectors, etc., are oversized for the job when delivering the same amount of power with 12 volts doing the pushing. (One of the side benefits that automobile manufacturers gained when they went over to 12-volt electrical systems was the opportunity to shave a bit off wire gauges, potentially saving a few pounds in weight and several bucks worth of copper.) So, the good news is that there is no need to change any wiring, switches, sockets, or fuses when up-rating an old system from 6 volts to 12, but you will have to replace the starter relay, all the bulbs, and the turn-signal flasher with 12-volt equivalents. Apart from the battery and the charging system (and we'll turn to that in a moment), that leaves only motors, relays, and instruments to worry about.

Though now common even on "bread-and-butter" cars, accessories that are powered or controlled by electricity—such as power windows and seats, air conditioning, and push-button heater and defroster controls—were rare until after the industry-wide conversion to 12-volt electrics in the mid-1950s, because of the already mentioned shortcomings of a 6-volt system. And what few did exist were generally restricted to vehicles at the top end of the market, where the bulk, weight, and cost of the oversized 6-volt generators and batteries they demanded could be justified. Accordingly, comparatively few motors and relays are to be found on most cars of the 6-volt era.

Twelve volts, in short, are better than 6.

Dropping Resistors ("Voltage Reducers")

The scarcity of motors and relays on a 6-volt system is fortunate because, while it is possible to adapt 6-volt relays and motors to 12-volt operation by using dropping resistors, the number of amps being drawn will be the same as in the original 6-volt system, despite the doubling of the source voltage. Using these resistors, in other words, will double the power consumed when the motor or relay is operated—one dose for the component, a second for the resistor, which turns its half of the supplied power into

heat. Happily, for a small number of components of comparatively low power consumption, or for units such as the horn that operates only momentarily, this should present no problem.

While the selection of an appropriate dropping resistor is fairly straightforward, it is vital to understand that there is no universal resistor that will convert 12 volts to 6. You have to establish the current draw of the component when operating from a 6-volt source, then arrange that the same current flows when it's supplied with 12.

Let's take the example of a windshield-wiper motor. First, establish the current draw of the motor when running on 6 volts. Assuming you have an ammeter that will cope with the expected current, connect it in series with the motor and a 6-volt battery, turn on the juice, and note and record the reading on the ammeter.

Be careful here: If you're using an inexpensive general purpose volt/ohm-meter, you'll likely find that its maximum capacity in the ammeter mode is less than 1 amp, sometimes much less. On the other hand, it probably won't be possible to read small currents with sufficient accuracy when using a conventional ammeter out of a car dashboard—it's a bit like trying to weigh a few ounces on a bathroom scale. If you haven't got access to a multiple-scale ammeter that can both cope with the current and give a clear reading, try the technique described in the sidebar Indirectly Measuring Large Currents with a Multi-Meter, in chapter eleven.

However you arrive at the answer, let's say you determine that the motor draws 2 amps. (Note, this must be done with the electric motor running, and under a representative load—let it be wiping a wet windshield; without any load, you'd be getting an unrealistically low reading for the current.)

Now, from Ohm's Law we can calculate the effective resistance of the motor:

6 volts/2 amps = 3 ohms

Because resistance in series simply adds up, we now know that we need to add a 3-ohm resistor in series with the motor, to bring the total resistance of the motor and resistor together up to 6 ohms. With 12 volts applied, the current will remain the same:

12 volts/6 ohms = 2 amps

(You shouldn't just assume that the battery voltage is exactly 6; you should separately measure the voltage across the battery terminals with the wiper motor running under load—it will almost certainly not be exactly 6 volts. Take this into account in your arithmetic.)

That's half the battle, but we also need to figure out how much *power* the resistor will be handling. Since a resistor "consumes" electrical power by turning it into heat, there is a limit to how much power a resistor can dissipate without overheating and burning out. Remember that power (in watts) is volts times amps. Since the whole object of the first calculation was to ensure that the same current would flow even though the voltage is doubled, we know that the current is 2 amps. But here's the slightly tricky part: What is the voltage? Considering the motor and the resistor together, it is certainly 12, but for the motor to "see" 6 volts, a 6-volt drop has to occur across the resistor. The resistor, then, will be dissipating power as follows:

2 amps x 6 volts = 12 watts

So, we need a 3-ohm, 12-watt resistor. In fact, to be on

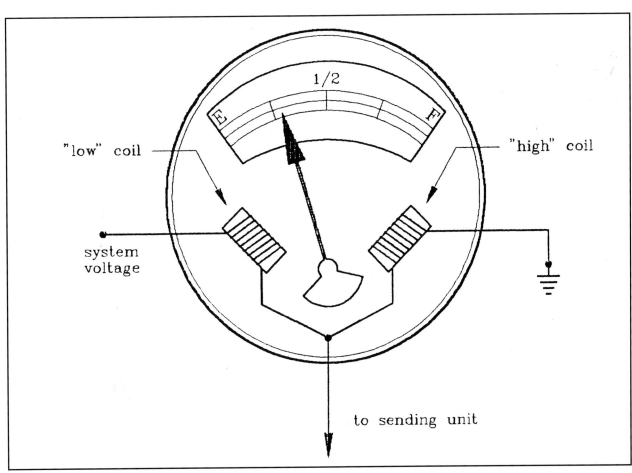

A balanced-coil-type gauge has an iron armature mounted on the needle. The armature is attracted to one side or the other, according to the relative current flow through each of two coils. System voltage is applied to both coils, but the amount of current that flows through each depends on the amount that flows to ground through the sending unit.

the safe side, a resistor rated at 15 watts or more would be preferable.

The only type of resistor that can dissipate this much heat (or, for that matter, the heat created almost anyplace else you might use one as part of a 6- to 12-volt adaptation) is the wire-wound type. As the name implies, it consists simply of a length of fine resistance wire, wound into a coil, which is exactly what you get if you buy one of the items sold to the old car community as voltage reducers.

Now, as noted above, there is no such thing as a resistor that will work as a universal voltage reducer, so it is hardly surprising that unsatisfactory results occur when these items are treated as a generic fix. When they work, it is because the resistance of the voltage reducer just happens to be right or close to right. When they don't, it is because the resistance is wrong.

The failure of these items to work as expected in certain sit-

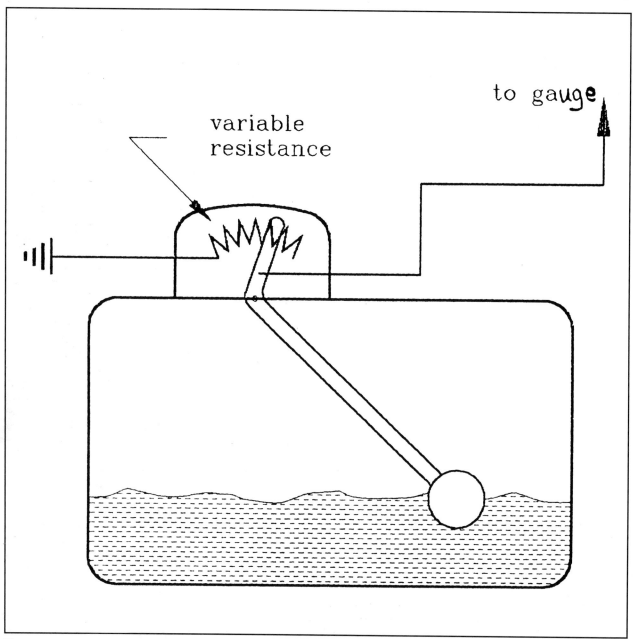

The sending unit for balanced coil-type gauges always takes the form of a variable resistor whose value changes according to the position of a mechanical wiper. In this typical fuel gauge application, the wiper arm takes up a position according to the height of the float riding on the surface of the gasoline.

90

uations is sometimes described as a matter of their "not getting hot enough." This is incorrect. Certainly the resistance of all resistors depends on their temperature, and their temperature depends on how much power they are dissipating. But the variation is very slight; even utility-grade wire-wound resistors vary in resistance no more than 100 parts per million (that's one part in 10,000) per degree of temperature rise. The difference between room temperature and literally red hot, then, is less than 10 percent, and a wire-wound resistor of the correct power rating will never get nearly that hot. Sure, if they aren't doing much "resisting," they will run cool. But the reason they're not working right isn't because they're too cool, it's simply because the resistance value is wrong.

A Theoretical Problem
In truth, the technique we have just described has a potentially serious theoretical drawback. The fact is, the resistance of an electric motor depends directly on its load, and that load is by no means steady. While it's easy to see that a wiper motor will work harder if the windshield is dry, or if it is covered with snow, even something like a heater-fan motor will vary in its current draw. The worst case is usually when the power first gets turned on because the inertia of the armature adds to the electrical load. This effect could make mincemeat out of any tidy calculation based on the current measured when the motor is under a steady-state load. What could happen, in theory, is this: The extra large current drawn by the motor when starting has to pass through the resistor; a large current through the resistor, however, means a correspondingly large voltage drop across the resistor. As a result, there may not be enough voltage to get the motor going! In practice this seldom

proves to be a problem, unless a combination of factors stacks up against you.

In practice, then, you can use this sort of calculation with confidence to establish the correct resistor for any 6-volt part that has a fixed resistance, such as a relay or a lamp. Components whose resistance varies, or where the applied voltage varies, present a greater challenge in theory, but you will usually get away with it.

Another example. The current flowing through the ignition coil varies according to engine speed and load. While it is some-

---

So, the good news is that there is no need to change any wiring, switches, sockets, or fuses when up-rating an old system from 6 volts to 12, but you will have to replace the starter relay, all the bulbs, and the turn-signal flasher.

---

times possible to get away with a simple dropping resistor to run a 6-volt coil from a 12-volt source, any single resistance will either cause a needlessly severe voltage drop just when you don't need it—while the starter is cranking, when the need for full rated voltage is most acute—or will permit an excessive current to flow at other times. Better you should use a 12-volt coil.

Instruments
Temperature and oil-pressure gauges on many cars from the pre-war era are purely mechanical, so they present no problem. Also, an ammeter is just that—it

measures amps—so it too can be left alone. Note, though, that you'll fry the ammeter if you put many more amps through it than the maximum value on the face. If you've got an ammeter that only reads to 30 amps and you install a monster alternator that puts out 50 or 60 amps, some day when your battery is pretty thoroughly discharged, that alternator is going to try to stuff its maximum output into the battery. And that current passes through the ammeter. *Fzzzzzt!* That doesn't just zap the ammeter, it also shuts off the entire electrical system, because everything (except for the current to the starter) goes through the ammeter. In many cases, then, there will be few electrically-operated instruments that need to be dealt with—perhaps just the fuel gauge.

The works in virtually all the electrically-operated gauges on cars boil down to one of two types. First is the balanced-coil movement. Inside the meter, there is a little iron slug connected to the shaft the pointer swivels on. Placed either side of this slug there are two small electromagnet coils. One coil is fed straight system voltage, so the current through it depends only on its own internal resistance; the other sees a current that varies according to the resistance of the sender unit. (In the case of a fuel gauge, for example, the sender unit consists of a float and lever arm that alters the resistance value of a variable resistor, according to the position of the float; other electrical sender units work in a similar way.) The pointer, then, takes up a position according to the strength of the magnetic field each coil develops, which in turn depends on the resistance of the sender unit.

Now, in principle, the balanced-coil arrangement should make such instruments quite insensitive to changes in system voltage. If they're any good, that's true, so converting from 6 volts to

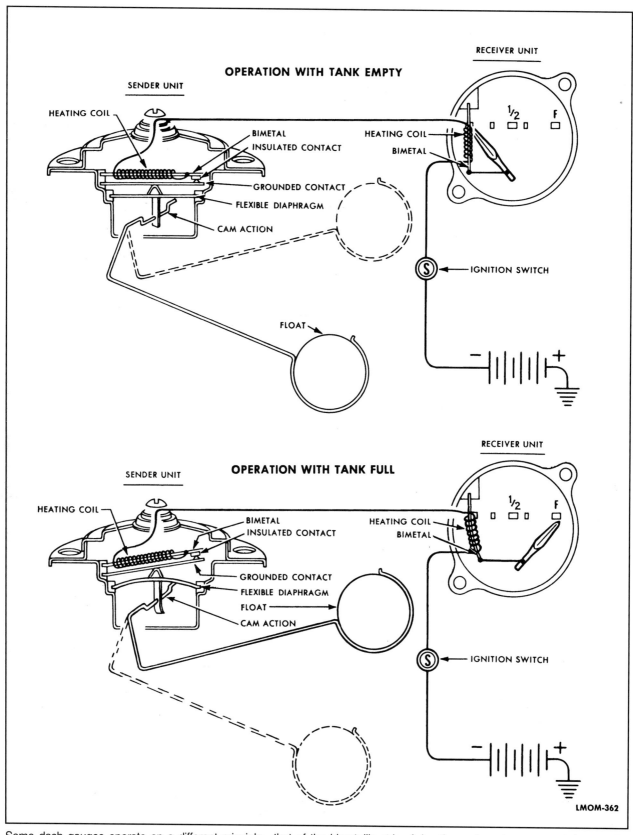

OPERATION WITH TANK EMPTY

RECEIVER UNIT

SENDER UNIT

HEATING COIL
BIMETAL
INSULATED CONTACT
GROUNDED CONTACT
FLEXIBLE DIAPHRAGM
CAM ACTION
FLOAT

HEATING COIL
BIMETAL
½   F
IGNITION SWITCH
−   +

OPERATION WITH TANK FULL

RECEIVER UNIT

SENDER UNIT

HEATING COIL
BIMETAL
INSULATED CONTACT
GROUNDED CONTACT
FLEXIBLE DIAPHRAGM
FLOAT
CAM ACTION

HEATING COIL
BIMETAL
½   F
IGNITION SWITCH
−   +

LMOM-362

Some dash gauges operate on a different principle—that of the bimetallic strip. A heating coil carries a current that, again, depends on the resistance of the sending unit. *Courtesy Ford Canada*

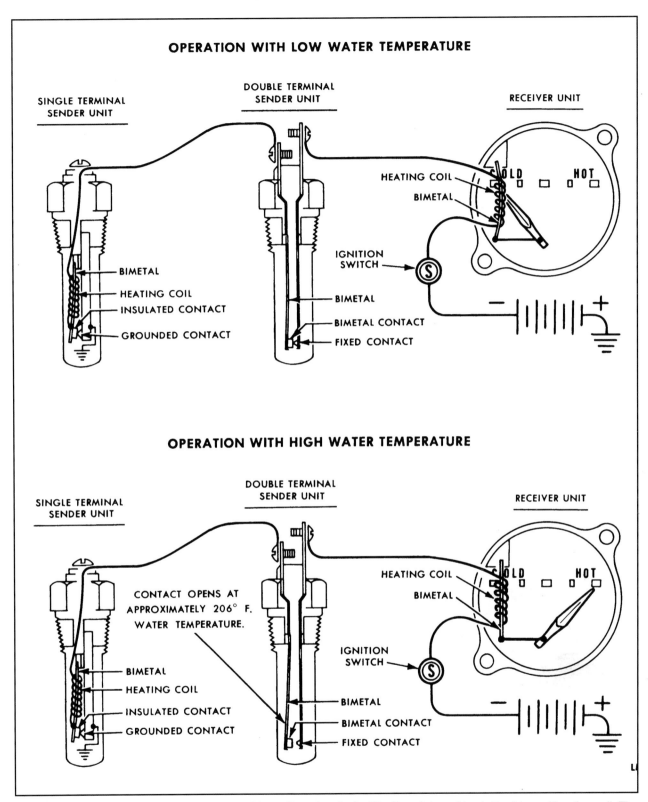

OPERATION WITH LOW WATER TEMPERATURE

SINGLE TERMINAL SENDER UNIT

DOUBLE TERMINAL SENDER UNIT

RECEIVER UNIT

HEATING COIL
BIMETAL
COLD HOT

BIMETAL
HEATING COIL
INSULATED CONTACT
GROUNDED CONTACT

IGNITION SWITCH

BIMETAL
BIMETAL CONTACT
FIXED CONTACT

OPERATION WITH HIGH WATER TEMPERATURE

SINGLE TERMINAL SENDER UNIT

DOUBLE TERMINAL SENDER UNIT

RECEIVER UNIT

HEATING COIL
BIMETAL
COLD HOT

CONTACT OPENS AT APPROXIMATELY 206° F. WATER TEMPERATURE.

IGNITION SWITCH

BIMETAL
HEATING COIL
INSULATED CONTACT
GROUNDED CONTACT

BIMETAL
BIMETAL CONTACT
FIXED CONTACT

The sending unit for a gauge operating on the bimetallic strip principal itself contains a bimetallic strip and heating coil. The physical variable being measured effectively varies the strength of the spring holding the current-carrying contacts closed. In this water temperature gauge, increasing temperature tends to hold the contacts shut longer, before the curvature of the bimetallic strip forces them open. That forces more current to flow, on average, through both the heating coil in the sender and the one in the gauge. *Courtesy Ford Canada*

93

12 shouldn't cause inaccurate readings. The problem is that the coils may burn out from the doubling of the current passing through them! We'll talk about how to deal with this in a moment.

The second type of electrically-operated gauge works on the principle of the bimetallic strip—the same kind of device that makes a turn-signal flasher switch itself on and off—that changes shape as its temperature changes, and so moves the needle on the gauge. The bimetallic strip is warmed by a small heating coil that is connected in series with the variable resistor that makes up the sending unit. To consider the fuel gauge, for instance, when the float moves lower as fuel is consumed, its resistance increases, so if a constant voltage is applied to the circuit, the current flowing through the heating coil diminishes. Less current means less heat, so the bimetallic strip cools somewhat, warps accordingly, and so moves the needle closer to the empty mark on the gauge face.

This principle of operation makes this type of instrument very sensitive to supply-voltage variations. Without close control over the supply voltage, a fuel gauge that reports a full tank of gas when the battery is fresh and the weather is warm, for example, might show "half" or less when the weather is cold and the battery is whacked out after a tough start. To avoid the inconvenience of gauges that tell you as much about the system voltage as they do about the thing they're actually supposed to indicate, some manufacturers installed instruments that run on a voltage somewhat lower than the nominal battery voltage and provided a device known as an "instrument voltage regulator," or IVR, to accurately maintain that lower voltage. The IVR takes the form of a little tin box found under the dash of some

cars from the beginning of the 12-volt era right up to the digital instrument era.

These IVRs themselves also frequently use a bimetallic strip and coil, just like the gauges they feed. Here, though, the change of shape of the strip when heated by the coil is used to open up a set of contact points, which shuts off the juice. The bimetallic strip then cools, re-establishing the contact, whereupon the whole cycle repeats. The points cycle open and shut more rapidly than the instruments can respond, and the average voltage output matches their requirements. Different makes and models vary in what that nominal

---

While the selection of an appropriate dropping resistor is fairly straightforward, it is vital to understand that there is no universal resistor that will convert 12 volts to 6.

---

value is, but most attempt to maintain just a bit over 5 volts, which is just fine for 6-volt balanced-coil instruments, of course; if a 6-volt bimetallic-type instrument seems slightly off kilter running off an IVR's regulated voltage, most such gauges have internal adjustments that allow a little fine tuning to bring them into line. Even more convenient (because unlike the OEM items they come with mounting tabs and spade connectors) are aftermarket IVRs. Blue Streak #VRC603 is an example. And something similar is available from Radio Shack as part #270-1562. This last has selectable outputs of 6 or 9 volts. (Incidentally, you can immediately tell

which type of instrument you're dealing with. The balanced-coil type will instantly flick to life as soon as the key is turned; the bimetallic type lazily works its way up to a steady reading, as the heating coil warms up.)

Dual-Voltage Systems

A final alternative solution to the complications of converting to 12 volts is to run a dual-voltage electrical system, with 12 volts supplied to whatever you want to run on 12 volts and 6 volts to the rest. In the case of older cars retaining the original engine, you might want to fit modern accessories, such as a tape deck, that come only in 12-volt versions, yet decide to leave the rest of the car with its original 6-volt equipment. Alternatively, you may want to fit a 12-volt ignition system and starter to gain improved reliability, especially in cold weather. In the case of modern engines installed into older chassis, there is no question of retaining authentic appearance, and anyway it would be sheer madness to convert the engine to 6-volt operation. Again, however, you may want to leave the rest of the electrical system as intact as possible.

One dual-voltage system of startling simplicity is to use a pair of 6-volt batteries, connected in series. A center tap from the cable connecting them feeds 6 volts to the starter and instruments, and any other component that's impractical to change; together, they supply 12 volts to everything else.

There are only two drawbacks to this arrangement: first, you have to find someplace to put the second battery; second, if the starter runs on 6 volts—i.e. just one battery—the battery that runs the starter will see much more severe service than the other one. As long as you aren't trying to fool a concours judge, the second battery can go in the trunk, under a seat, or anyplace

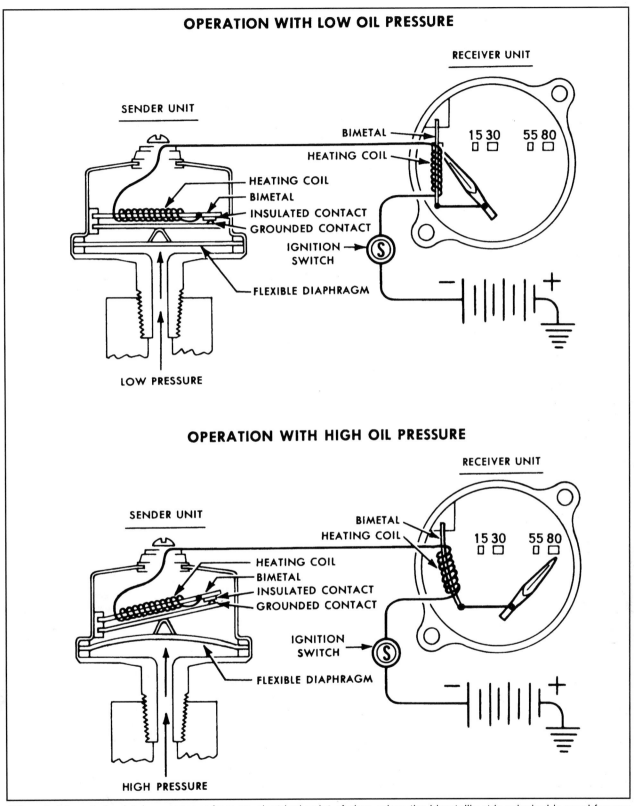

OPERATION WITH LOW OIL PRESSURE

RECEIVER UNIT

SENDER UNIT

BIMETAL

HEATING COIL

15 30   55 80

HEATING COIL
BIMETAL
INSULATED CONTACT
GROUNDED CONTACT

IGNITION
SWITCH

FLEXIBLE DIAPHRAGM

–   +

LOW PRESSURE

OPERATION WITH HIGH OIL PRESSURE

RECEIVER UNIT

SENDER UNIT

BIMETAL
HEATING COIL

15 30   55 80

HEATING COIL
BIMETAL
INSULATED CONTACT
GROUNDED CONTACT

IGNITION
SWITCH

FLEXIBLE DIAPHRAGM

–   +

HIGH PRESSURE

Although it is not absolutely necessary from an electrical point of view, when the bimetallic strip principal is used for one electric dash gauge, it is generally used for all of them. While the internal construction of the different gauges may be identical, a different arrangement is required for the sending unit, as can be seen by comparing this oil pressure gauge with the previous picture of a temperature gauge operating on the same principle. *Courtesy Ford Canada*

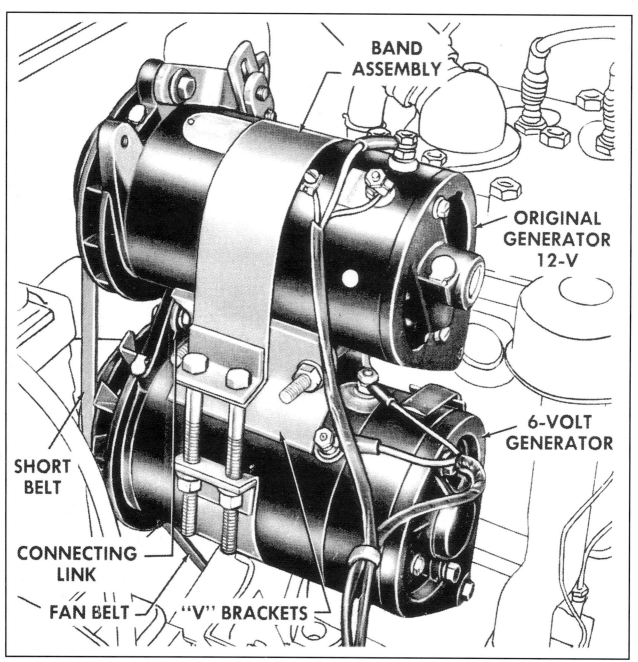

BAND ASSEMBLY

ORIGINAL GENERATOR 12-V

6-VOLT GENERATOR

SHORT BELT

CONNECTING LINK

FAN BELT

"V" BRACKETS

For a time in the 1950s and 1960s, dual-voltage charging systems were offered for specialty applications. Though most of these were intended to add a 6-volt generator to an existing 12-volt system, there's no reason you can't apply the same principle the other way around. Delco shows how. *Courtesy GM Canada*

else physical space is available—but beware of the voltage drop incurred by such long cables. The problem of widely differing demands on the two batteries is a little trickier.

Obviously, the starter-duty battery will undergo much deeper discharge cycles than the other one, so will tend to age faster for that reason. On the other hand, there will be a tendency for the second battery to be overcharged, as the 12-volt generator (or alternator) puts out lots of amps trying to get the starter-duty battery back up to charge after a bout of heavy cranking. A little thought

in arranging the battery cables should make it possible to swap the connections around from time to time—say weekly—to help to average out these differing demands. Alternatively, you can swap the batteries themselves.

A variation on this dual-voltage theme that deals with the

above problem is to arrange to connect the batteries in series for 12 volts, or in parallel for 6. This could be done with a jumper cable arrangement, but far more convenient is a relay-operated series/parallel switch.

One supplier listed in Appendix B offers an "automatic" 6/12-volt battery that actually consists of two small 6-volt batteries in one case, together with a relay-operated switch that normally connects the two sections of the battery in parallel to provide 6 volts to most of the vehicle, but couples them in series to feed just the starter when the relay is energized by the starter switch. The relay-operated series/parallel switch may be available separately. Note that this arrangement supplies 12 volts to the starter, but six to the car—this is not a solution that applies if you want to convert part or all of the rest of the car to 12-volt operation.

On such as a street rod, where a late-model (12-volt) engine has been transplanted into a 6-volt-era chassis, it obviously makes sense to leave all the engine electrics alone; one or several of the solutions described above should take care of adapting the rest of the car. Where this is not the case, that is, when the engine was originally equipped with 6-volt electrics but it is desired to change the vehicle over to 12, a remaining unsolved problem is the starter.

Starting on Twelve Volts
Apart from a dual-voltage system, as described, there are three courses of action in this case. First, you can try to find a 12-volt starter motor that is a bolt-on replacement for the original 6-volt unit. This may prove practical with engines that were built over the transition period. Overhead-valve Ford Y-block V-8s, flathead Chryco sixes, and Chev and GM "stove-bolt" sixes, for example, existed both before and after the companies switched to

12 volts. Some later starters will bolt on to earlier engines. In other cases, and almost certainly if the engine dates from before World War II, such a bolt-on swap may prove impossible to find (internal parts may be interchangeable, however).

The second solution is to get the field windings in the starter re-wound for 12-volt operation. If you can't find a local auto electrical shop willing to take this on, there are a number of specialist firms that will do this sort of work. The drawback to this approach is your dependence on a very rare starter motor. What do you do when miles from home and the starter craps out?

Temperature and oil-pressure gauges on many cars from the pre-war era are purely mechanical, so they present no problem. Also, an ammeter is just that—it measures amps—so it too can be left alone.

The third solution, then: Do nothing! Run the original 6-volt starter on 12 volts. This sounds like it must be murder on the starter, but the fact is that many, many 6-volt starters live quite happily on a 12-volt diet for years. (The writer can personally attest to a Ford flathead starter that survived this treatment for at least six years without complaint.) In fact, if you were to hand an automotive starter to an electrical engineer and ask him to rate its working voltage, he would come up with an answer of a couple of volts. That's because the limiting factor in rating electric motors is the temperature-

tolerance limit of the insulation and the internal soldered connections; conventional industrial ratings for the power of a DC motor (and so of voltage) are based on the internal temperatures reached during continuous operation. As long as you don't let the starter grind away for minute after minute, the temperature rise will stay within the motor's tolerance, even when the voltage is doubled. If you exceed the thermal limit of the starter, the most likely result will be "thrown solder"—the combination of overheating and centrifugal force will melt the solder and separate the armature segments.

If you fit a 12-volt starter, and it is the type with a separate, firewall-mounted relay, you will need a 12-volt starter relay. (Alternatively, you could fit a dropping resistor to an existing 6-volt relay. The coil in the relay has a fixed resistance, so this is one place where the selection of the value for the dropping resistor is straightforward. Just follow the procedure described in the previous chapter, and don't forget to figure the wattage rating you need when selecting the resistor.)

An unmodified 6-volt relay *will* switch 12 volts—remember, the contacts inside it are limited in the amperage they will carry, not the voltage—but the doubling of the current through the *coil* in the relay will cause it to overheat. As a result, in the worst case, the relay may wind up stuck in the on position, with the starter whizzing away, maybe munching up itself and the ring gear, even though you've let off on the switch.

Twelve-Volt Charging
On the charging side, you will need a 12-volt alternator or generator. If you are concerned about retaining original appearance, or keeping close to it, you may seek out a 12-volt generator that is a bolt-on replacement for the original 6-volt unit. This will prove

This dual-voltage battery is simply two small 6-volt units in one case, with a center tap for the 6-volt connection. *Courtesy Antique Auto Battery Manufacturing Co.*

One dual-voltage system of startling simplicity is to use a pair of 6-volt batteries, connected in series. A center tap from the cable connecting them feeds 6 volts to the starter and instruments, and any other component that's impractical to change; together, they supply 12 volts to everything else.

easier for vehicles built during the last few years of the 6-volt era, but compared to starters, generators are easier to adapt to new surroundings. Do not overlook the opportunity to choose a generator with a greater than original output, but be sure you use a matching regulator. In the case of flathead Fords, the original generator can be rebuilt using a 12-volt armature and field coils.

You will also need a 12-volt regulator that is well matched to that generator. Remember that the mechanical regulators used with generators have three coils—one for voltage to keep the battery happy, a cut-out to pre-vent the battery discharging itself to ground through the generator, and a coil that limits the current output of the generator to prevent it from destroying itself if it should face too large a load. You must be sure that the current setting on the regulator will protect your generator.

Since we're talking about conversions here, you may have given up on any notion of authenticity. In that case, an alternator seems the most reasonable choice. The regulator is built right into the alternator on all current vehicles, but if you have an alternator from the comparatively brief period when they came with a sepa-rate, remote-mounted regulator, you will need the regulator that was designed to run with that specific alternator.

About the only other complication is the issue of polarity—whether the car was originally positive ground or negative ground. All modern cars are negative ground, but many older ones, especially older ones with 6-volt systems, were positive ground. In these cases, when you're converting the car to 12 volts, you will have to change it to negative ground at the same time. This is dealt with in the next chapter.

The third solution, then: Do nothing! Run the original 6-volt starter on 12 volts. This sounds like it must be murder on the starter, but the fact is that many, many 6-volt starters live quite happily on a 12-volt diet for years.

The same thing is available with a parallel/series relay switch, to feed 12 volts to just the starter, when the starter relay is energized by the starter switch, and 6 volts to everything else. *Courtesy Antique Auto Battery Manufacturing Co.*

Polarity and Grounds

9

Designers over the years have had mixed opinions about whether the positive or negative terminal of the battery should be the ground, the other one obviously being the hot lead. This choice is what is meant by polarity. Every modern car is negative ground—it is the negative terminal of the battery that is connected to the vehicle chassis—and this has been the arrangement used on almost all domestic makes since the switch to 12-volt systems in the middle 1950s. Before that, however, most vehicles had positive-ground electrics. As a general rule, then, 6-volt cars are positive ground and 12-volt ones are negative ground. But there are plenty of exceptions to this general rule. The 1955 Packards used a 12-volt positive-ground system, for instance, as did some (but not all) 1953–1955 Chryslers. And many 6-volt GM cars used negative ground.

Also, most English cars that made their way to these shores had 12-volt positive-ground systems made by the English company Lucas. A reason offered for this arrangement was a theoretical argument about the nature of the spark at the plug. Without getting into the theory, the basic claim was that a positive-ground system made for easier starting. Anyone who has ever dealt with an early Lucas electrical system will get a laugh from that!

If you are converting a 6-volt positive-ground car to 12-volt operation, you should certainly change to negative ground at the same time. Obviously, this will allow you to use any modern electrical accessories, such as a tape player, but the major reason for this recommendation is the opportunity to fit a conventional, negative-ground 12-volt alternator. (There are a few positive-ground alternators around, offered by some of the small companies that cater to the old-car specialty trade, but for obscure reasons these positive-ground alternators are usually not "self-exciting." Because of that, they have to be spun up to about 1,500 engine rpm before they will start to charge, which seriously detracts from one of the primary advantages of an alternator over a generator—the ability to put out a useful charging current when the engine is idling.)

If you are converting a 6-volt positive-ground car to 12-volt operation, you should certainly change to negative ground at the same time.

If you have one of those rarities—a 12-volt positive-ground car—then about the only good reason to change to negative ground is because you want to fit modern accessories or a modern electronic ignition system (see chapter five) that will only operate as part of a negative-ground system. Likewise, you may want to change a 6-volt positive-ground car to 6 volts negative ground for similar reason(s), using some variation on the dual-voltage scheme described in the previous chapter. (Note that you can't have a dual-voltage system that provides 6 volts positive ground and 12 volts negative ground.)

Polarity Conversion

To perform the polarity conversion, you will have to re-arrange the battery cables, so the negative post is the one connected to ground and the positive post connects to the starter solenoid. (Obviously, you should leave the battery disconnected until you've completed the swap.) The primary leads on the coil will have to be switched around, too; the wire that connects to the distributor should be connected to the "-" terminal. If the engine is equipped with a DC generator, you next have to polarize the generator. What's happening is that the pole shoes—the soft-iron cores—inside the field coils retain some degree of permanent magnetism. Since all the north and south poles need to get switched around, you have to overwhelm that residual magnetism with a shot of electromagnetism going the "right" way. To do that, briefly touch the hot (positive) lead from the battery to the "Field" terminal on the generator. That reverses the polarity of the pole shoes.

About the only other major thing you have to attend to is the regulator; the cores in its internal coils will also have taken on a permanent magnetic set. Assuming you're dealing with a mechanical-type regulator, briefly touch the lead coming from the "Field" terminal of the regulator to the "Bat" terminal, before hooking things up permanently. There's another potential problem, though. While most mechanical regulators are universal—they will work just as well in negative- or positive-ground systems, as long as they are polarized in the way described—there are some found on older 6-volt cars that are sensitive to the polarity. To improve the life of the contact points in the regulator, their manufacturers made the two contact points out of different metals; even if correctly polarized, these points will burn out rapidly when the current flow is reversed. This only applies to 6-volt vehicles, anyway, and it is not likely you will be changing the polarity unless you are also using a 12-volt charging system. If you are, though, and if you are unsure about the nature of the regulator, you will have to replace it with a universal 6-volt unit.

Finally, if you're running an ammeter, you should also reverse its leads, otherwise it will read backwards, which doesn't hurt anything but can be confusing. While you're at it, remember our previous caution about being sure the ammeter can carry the full output of the charging system—a 50-amp generator (or alternator) will kill an ammeter that only reads to 30 amps.

Grounds

We have previously explained that electricity has to have a complete path, or circuit, in order to flow: You can't just feed a single wire from a battery to any electrical device and have it work; you need a second connection leading back from the device to the other terminal of the battery. In automobiles the second, return path—called the ground—is formed by the metal body and chassis of the car. Although iron and steel do not conduct as well as copper, there is so much of it that there is only one serious objection to this practice—rust!

When iron or steel is exposed to the air, some of the material at the surface immediately combines with some of the oxygen in the atmosphere to form iron oxide, commonly called rust. Iron and steel also readily combine with other chemicals in the atmosphere, such as acids from engine exhaust and salt from winter snow-clearing operations. What's more, when iron is in close contact with another metal and the joint is exposed even to damp air, yet another type of corrosion goes to work, filling the connection with some new material. Now, while iron conducts pretty well, these products of corrosion

---

Manufacturers are extremely stingy when it comes to copper wire. Apart from selecting the skinniest cable that will do the job, they invest a lot of time and effort planning the shortest possible routes for wiring and battery cables.

---

do not, so it is hardly surprising that the electrical systems of older cars behave as if they are full of bad connections—they are!

As we mentioned in chapter seven, manufacturers are extremely stingy when it comes to copper wire. Apart from selecting the skinniest cable that will do the job, they invest a lot of time and effort planning the shortest possible routes for wiring and battery cables. One example of this mentioned in chapter seven is the usual "bass-ackward" method of forming the ground return for the starter—by far the heaviest current draw in the

vehicle. The battery ground post is usually connected to the nearest point on the frame or body, so to get from the starter housing to the battery ground post, the current has to pass through the engine, through a ground strap from there to the frame, then through a whole bunch of joints in sheet metal, etc., to the place where the battery ground strap connects to the frame or body.

Bad as it is, this is a pretty direct route compared with the path from, say, a taillight back to the battery ground post. The current has to travel through one or more joints between the taillight housing and the fender, from the fender to the rear of the body, through various connections between body panels all the way to the front of the car, where it reaches the bolt that secures the battery ground strap, then finally through the strap to the battery ground post. Often, one panel is insulated from another by rubber gaskets, so that the only electrical path is through the threads on bolts or sheet-metal screws. While this invisible ground path may work adequately well when the car is new, the resistance grows over time as these connections corrode. That's when you get the weird symptoms, such as turn signals that stop blinking when you press on the brakes. What's usually happening here is that, because of a bad ground connection, one bulb grounds itself through the filament of another.

Ironically, the very act of restoring the body work of an old car can make the situation even worse, as paint replaces rust. The headlights in lovingly restored buckets may refuse to light when the housing is bolted to the fender; a freshly painted bracket for a horn may result in asthmatic squawks, or even complete silence from the horn.

Take heart, though: This problem is another example of our rule that all of what goes wrong in vehicle electrical systems (as opposed to electronic systems) is essentially mechanical. There are two approaches. One is to restore solid, metal-to-metal connections in the chassis ground—the invisible ground wire—all the way from the component back to the battery post. This method argues for sanding *all* the metal clean, then assembling the body completely, and only then painting it. No? Don't like the idea of all that rust starting all over again in the invisible places?

In chapter seven, we suggested that the solution to the usual fouled-up starter ground was to run a suitable conductor from one of the starter mounting bolts directly to the ground post of the battery. You can do the same thing with other components. You could run a separate ground wire, of the same gauge as the supply wire, from each headlight, taillight, etc., directly back to the battery. (If you are building up your own wiring harness, avoid the temptation to build the ground wires in; if there is anyplace within the harness where that extra wire can contact a 'hot' lead—such as when somebody sticks the sharp end of a test probe into the bundle and nails them both at the same time—you've got an instant short circuit, and possibly a fire.)

An alternative is to run a ground bus, or several of them, that serve as a secure ground for components in various parts of the car. One hefty wire (say #6 or #8 gauge) could be run to the rear of the car, to service all the lights there; another to the area of the headlights and parking lamps at the front for them to use as a ground. Each of these bus wires should connect directly to the battery ground post. Un-insulated wire will rapidly corrode, so insulated wire should be used, even though a ground return doesn't need to be insulated for electrical purposes—it's already a ground. For the same reason, it doesn't matter if there's incidental contact between them and the frame or body.

Wiring

10

We think nothing of the occasional need to fit new regulators, ignition points, condensers, and coils. Experience has also taught us that batteries gradually lose performance over time and need replacement at intervals of a few years. Likewise, most people accept that starters and generators get tuckered out with age, and that they can and should be revived, as necessary, by re-machining their commutators and installing new brushes and bearings. It is less widely appreciated, however, that wire itself deteriorates with the passage of time. Indeed, it is by no means uncommon for a restoration job to involve refurbishment or replacement of virtually every part of a vehicle, *except* its wiring. Alas, it is possible to point at instances where funky old wiring has caused the total loss of, or at least extensive damage to, an otherwise fully-restored vehicle.

There are two reasons why we should be skeptical about old wiring. First is the integrity of the insulation. Very early wiring, say pre-World War II, will have insulation made of natural rubber, usually covered with varnished fabric. The cover provides some abrasion resistance but seems mostly to exist as a means of color-coding individual wires—natural rubber comes only in black! Synthetic rubber (Neoprene) came later, to be replaced in turn by a variety of plastics, which eventually became tough enough that the fabric cover could be deleted. Exposure to heat, light, and ozone takes its toll on all these materials, causing them to become brittle; rubber, especially, hardens and eventually turns to a crumbly powder with age, exposing bare wire. Obviously, anyplace the conductor is unprotected is a potential source of a short circuit.

The second area of concern is the copper wire itself. While it is an excellent conductor of electricity, copper is also a fairly reactive metal, and it will readily combine with an assortment of elements, including oxygen in the atmosphere. Now, copper is

If your primary concern is a reliable electrical system, and you are prepared to sacrifice authentic appearance, it is quite possible to construct your own wiring harness, saving some money in the process.

expensive, so the designers of the vehicle will have provided no more than is necessary to do the job. If some of that copper has since turned into copper oxide or copper sulfate, there is now less conductor to carry the current. That increases resistance, which increases heat, which in turn increases the rate of decay of both the wire and the insulation. And even if the conductor itself is little affected, every junction where a wire is connected to a terminal is an interface between dissimilar metals—a place where corrosion can do its foul work. In short, if the wiring is older than you are, it is probably in bad shape.

Completely re-wiring a car can be an intimidating task, made all the more daunting when it is desired to maintain an authentic, original appearance. Because many of the factors that cause wiring to deteriorate apply even when the parts are sitting on a shelf, NOS wiring should be shunned. Fortunately, there are a number of specialist services offering complete wiring looms for many older cars, using modern, plastic-insulated wire, overwrapped, where historically appropriate, with lacquered fabric in original patterns and colors. If your object is authentic, original appearance, this route—albeit expensive—is the only one available.

If, however, your primary concern is a safe and reliable electrical system, and you are prepared to sacrifice absolutely authentic appearance, it is quite possible to construct your own wiring harness, saving some money in the process. Similarly, if you have an "orphan" vehicle, the cost of a custom-fabricated, original-appearing loom may be prohibitive (though note that some of the businesses mentioned above will, for a price, apply a braided fabric loom around a customer-supplied wiring harness). Buying a ready-made loom, however, does not eliminate all the effort of re-wiring. While making a complete wiring harness may seem like a large amount of work, in many cases the hardest part of the job is removing the original wiring and installing the finished replacement.

The task of manufacturing a replacement wiring harness is greatly eased if there is an original to copy. It is customary for the wiring of a car to be broken down into sections. Often, there are three major groupings—one under the hood, one extending through the passenger compartment, and a third running from somewhere around the rear-seat bulkhead, feeding the lamps at the back end. More modern cars may have several sub-harnesses serving separate areas or systems, such as the dashboard instruments. Remove all these with care, noting what goes where, and labeling everything in sight. Careful taking of notes and drawing of diagrams can prevent much grief later.

Depending on the make, model, and age of car, the individual sections may end in very specialized multi-pin connectors that plug onto through-fittings secured to the firewall and rear bulkhead. It may be possible to dismantle these connectors to allow separation of the wires and re-use of the terminals. In other cases it will be possible to fish the wire terminal ends out of the plastic body of the connector. If these are of a type for which replacements are available, they can simply be chopped off and discarded; otherwise it may be necessary to carefully un-crimp the individual connectors for re-use. And some of the same suppliers that offer complete wiring harnesses for older cars can also provide NOS or reproduction connectors. If original or reproduction

connectors are unavailable, or unaffordable, generic multi-pin connectors are available from various suppliers that will achieve the same purpose, though at the expense of original appearance. As an alternative to multi-pin connectors, or in addition to them, individual wires can be terminated with soldered or solderless (crimped) connectors.

Choosing Wire

The wire itself must be appropriate for the job. The only wire that should be considered has a copper conductor and is made specifically for automotive, marine, or light-aircraft use—household lamp cord and hi-fi speaker hookup wire are right out! (Don't laugh—both have been used.) The critical points are that the wire be copper, multi-stranded, of

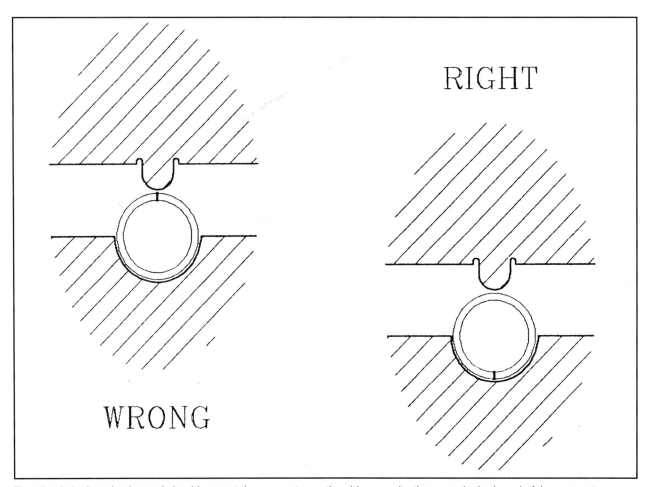

RIGHT

WRONG

The dimple in the crimping tool should contact the connector on the side opposite the seam in the barrel of the connector.

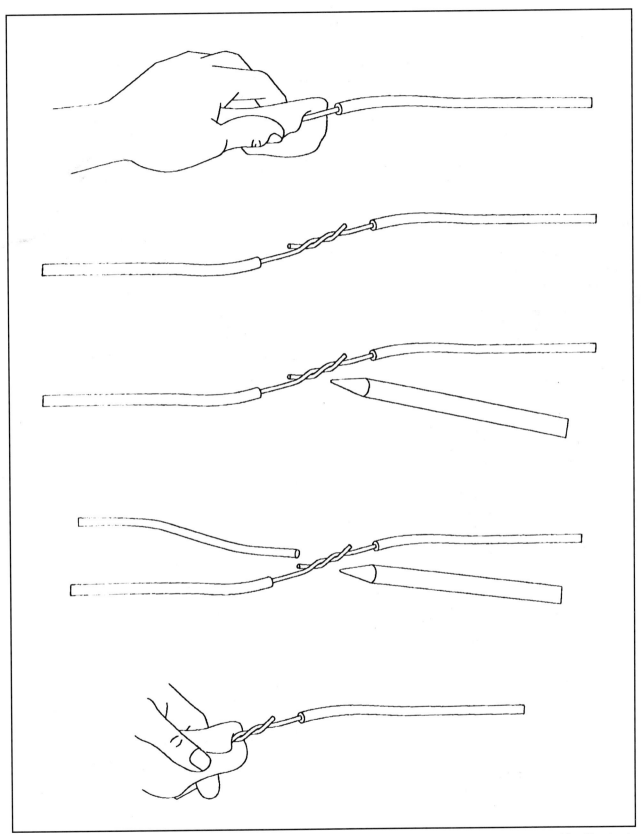

The main trick when soldering is to use the iron to heat the wire, not the solder. Despite the use of resin-core solder, it's wise to apply flux to the wire ends before joining, and to clean off the excess flux when you're done. *Courtesy Cooper Tools*

the correct gauge, and with an appropriate insulation. (You may encounter wire using an aluminum or stainless-steel conductor. Both are cheaper than copper; neither is as suitable.)

Single-strand wire, in which the conductor is one solid piece—as used in many electronics and household applications—is completely unsuitable. It is not flexible enough to cope with the vibrations of an operating automobile without fracturing. Also, the many fine strands that make up multi-strand wire offer increased contact area at the terminals, whether crimped or soldered. Note, though, that not all multi-strand wire is the same—#18-gauge wire could have 7 or 19 or 41 strands. Generally speaking, more strands means greater flexibility, and so better vibration resistance.

The gauge of a wire refers to the diameter of the conductor; smaller numbers mean a larger diameter. As we have seen in chapter one, the fatter the conductor, the lower the resistance. Don't get confused, here, by the outside diameter of the insulation. A spark plug wire, for instance, can be called on to handle 30,000 volts or more, so it has very thick insulation to prevent breakdown and arcing. On the other hand, the current is extremely small, so only a very thin conductor is needed. A battery cable, by contrast, deals with just 12 (or 6) volts, so its insulation need be no thicker than that needed to avoid tearing and abrasion; however, to keep resistance to a minimum while carrying 200 or 300 amps, the conductor itself is as thick as your finger.

If an existing harness is available for comparison, the existing wires will serve as a guide—though only a guide—to choosing the gauges of their

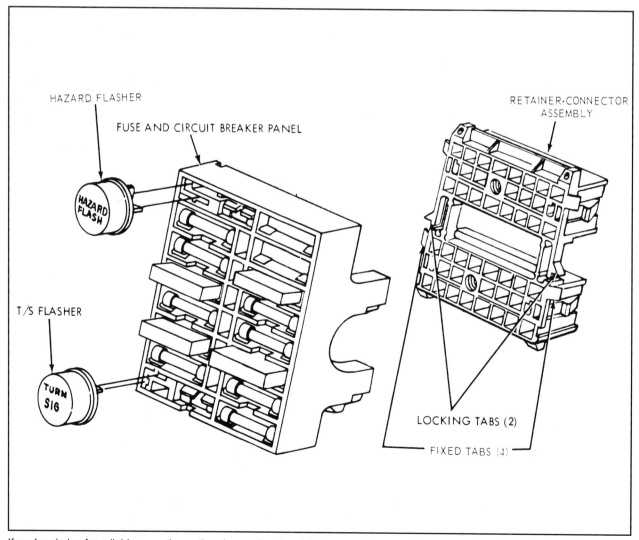

If you're aiming for reliable operation, rather than authentic original appearance, you can scrounge a fuse/terminal block from any modern car. Many of these also make provision for a turn signal flasher. *Courtesy Ford Canada*

replacements. As already noted, factory-original wiring will be of the smallest gauge that will do the job, so while you should never go smaller than the original, there is a good argument for going one gauge larger. (In fact, the only practical upper limit to wire gauge is the problem of physical bulk.)

If you are going to increase the electrical load on a circuit, say by installing brighter bulbs, or you intend to build in an extra circuit to supply a new feature, such as a radio, you should carefully consider the maximum load on that circuit. Once the load is known, and the length of the wire is measured or calculated, the correct gauge of wire can be established by consulting Table 1 or 2. Again, these are *minimum* gauges; it does no harm to go one size larger. It is also worth noting that a certain amount of heat is created by the resistance of marginally sized wiring; while this will not be a problem with individual wires, it can become a problem when multiple wires are packed closely together in a harness (see Table 3 in appendix A)—another argument for being conservative when specifying wire gauges.

A final point about the conductor itself. At a substantial cost premium, wire is available that is "pre-tinned"—each strand has been separately plated with tin. This greatly reduces the risk of corrosion and makes for more secure soldered joints; tinned copper wire is used in marine and aviation applications, for just those reasons. Although ordinary automotive wire is adequate (provided it is multi-strand copper), it's worth noting a couple of specs for pre-tinned wire.

Strange as it may seem, while there are a great many MIL-spec numbers and other identifiers for "aircraft" wire, the Federal Aviation Administration (FAA) provides no explicit definition for the stuff. Nevertheless,

the FAA does demand "best industry practice," and lists a number of specs that meet their standards. Of these, the one most closely applicable to automotive re-wiring is MIL-W-22759/26. This has a tinned-copper, multi-strand conductor, and insulation good to 300 degrees F. It is available in 15 sizes from #02 gauge (0.4575-inch nominal conductor outside diameter) through #24 gauge (0.0235-inch outside diameter).

Although a car, especially a collectible car, is not likely to be operated in a salt-water environment, boats are. The materials and techniques used by marine electrical specialists, then, can be expected to represent the state of the art in guarding against the hazards of corrosion in electrical wiring systems. When it comes to wire, the American Boat and Yacht Council recommends tinned, multi-strand copper conductors. Top-line yacht builders agree, accepting the 20–40 percent cost premium for the material in exchange for corrosion resistance that is two-and-a-half to three times that of bare copper.

The final consideration in choosing wire is the insulation. The first plastic replacements for fabric and rubber insulation were *thermoplastics*, such as PVC and vinyl—materials that soften when heated and harden again when cooled. Without getting into the specifics of the extensive variety of these materials, some of which are still widely used for wire insulation, it is generally fair to say that they have less tear resistance and lower service-temperature limits than the more modern *cross-linked thermoset* plastics. For most applications it simply doesn't matter what kind of plastic the insulation is made from, and the selection can be made on the basis of cost and the variety of colors available. Where heat may be a problem, however, such as for wiring that has to run near an exhaust manifold, the

roughly 185-degree limit of typical over-the-parts-counter automotive wiring may be inadequate. Insulation of Kynar or polyolefin is serviceable to 250 degrees; the MIL-W-22759/26-spec wire, noted above, has Tefzel insulation good for a hair over 300 degrees; Teflon will tolerate nearly 400 degrees.

Finally, as to colors, the trick is to have enough different colors on hand to avoid hopeless confusion, without having to purchase absurdly large quantities of wire. About the only inflexible rule is that you should use one consistent color for all wires leading to ground; green or black are conventionally used for this purpose. It may be tempting to use a different color for the "same" wire in different sections of the harness, to provide a wider selection within any one section, so helping to keep straight what goes where. At the least, this will make your notes and diagrams a bit more complicated; at worst it can lead to wholesale confusion. Better you should pony up for an extra roll of wire of a different color. (Of course, there is a limit to the number of different colors that can be told apart at a glance, especially in dim light, and this total is likely to be smaller than the number of circuits that you want to separately identify. To provide a greater variety, wires also come with a thin line, or "tracer," of a different color.)

Whatever the wire, the next task is cutting a new length to duplicate each piece in the original, a job that requires no talents beyond patience and care. When stripping the insulation off the wire ends, though, it is vital to use a tool designed for the job. Pen knives, utility knives, razor blades, etc., all risk nicking the fine strands of conductor. Use a proper wire-stripping tool, preferably one that has separate notches for different gauges, rather than the adjustable "one-size-fits-all" type. (See chapter eleven.)

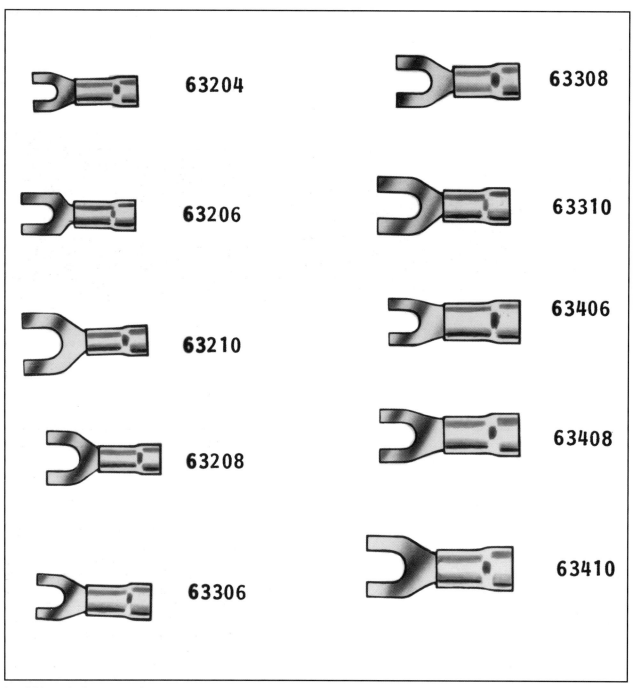

In addition to bell-mouth end terminals like these, solderless connectors are available with spade ends—both male and female—and with ring and other type fittings. *Courtesy Klein Tools*

Even if you are using factory multi-pin connectors for the major connections, there will be many places where single, individual connectors are needed. For convenience of initial assembly at the factory, and for ease of servicing later, matching male and female quick-disconnect connectors are commonly used. Though these seldom cause trouble, wherever practical it is better to use ring-type connectors that completely surround the stud or screw that secures them.

Soldering Versus Crimping

Then comes the matter of connecting the wire ends to the terminals. There are two schools of thought here. One argues that a properly soldered connection is more electrically sound than any

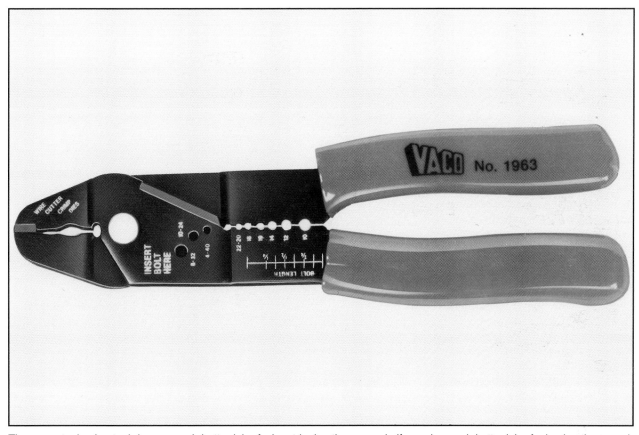

The correct crimping tool does a much better job of wire stripping than a penknife, and a much better job of crimping than a pair of pliers. *Courtesy Klein Tools*

crimped connector because there is so much more metal-to-metal contact between the conductor (the wire) and the barrel or sleeve of the terminal. Also, say the advocates of soldering, the risk of corrosion inside the joint is eliminated because the space is completely filled with solder, so no moisture can get in.

The other school claims that not only is solder unnecessary, it is positively harmful. The reasoning is that a correctly crimped solderless connector is virtually failure-proof—certainly better than a fouled-up solder job—and it is easier for the average person to do a proper job of crimping than it is to produce a satisfactory soldered joint. The clincher, say these folks, is that solder that "wicks" along the strands of wire in the conductor produces a stiff region that can

lead to fracturing under vibration, right at the point where the solder ends.

Though both theories have merit, both also leave room for disagreement. On the one hand, solder is not a particularly good electrical conductor; on the other, there is something slightly fishy about the "stiff area" argument. First, there is a fairly abrupt change in stiffness anyway, right where the wire is crimped into the solderless connector. Second, if the entire job is done in a professional manner, the wires should be physically supported, to prevent vibration being focused at the joint. Certainly it is a bad idea to depend on solder to provide a mechanical link, so crimp-type connectors should be used (and crimped!) even if you decide to use solder. Although solder is soft, it is unreasonable

to expect it to cold-flow satisfactorily during the crimping, so the soldering should be done afterwards, not before.

You would think that it would be hard to go wrong with something as apparently stone-ax simple as solderless connectors, yet there are a surprising number of ways to foul up. First is the matter of size.

Solderless connectors are made in different sizes to accommodate different gauges of wire, though it is usual for each size of connector to serve two different wire gauges. These connectors are available in both insulated and uninsulated types. If you intend to solder, you will want uninsulated connectors; the best of these have pre-tinned barrels. (If uninsulated connectors are not readily available, the insulating sleeve can easily be cut off the insulated type.) To provide insulation and physical support, and to seal the joint, a piece of heat-shrink tubing, sometimes called "spaghetti," should be fitted over the end of the wire (before forming the connection!), then slipped over the exposed joint before being shrunk into place. The heat for the shrinking can come from a match, cigarette lighter, heat gun, or soldering iron. Although the spaghetti will be unaffected by a brief application of a flame, an open flame represents a distinct fire hazard; when working on the car, and especially under the dash or in other confined quarters, a heat source that doesn't involve an open flame is far safer. Note, too, that the heat-shrink tubing must be pushed well away from the joint during soldering, so it is not prematurely shrunk by the heat.

For the insulated connectors, there is a color code used fairly consistently by the manufacturers of these things—red insulation for #18 or #20 gauge, blue for #14 or #16 gauge, and yellow for #10 or #12 gauge.

Now, it's hard to get into trouble by mistakenly installing a #10-gauge wire into a red connector designed for #18/20-gauge wire—it simply won't fit. You might be tempted, though, to try it the other way around, slipping a skinny #18-gauge wire into a yellow (#10/12-gauge) connector.

You would think that it would be hard to go wrong with something as apparently stone-ax simple as solderless connectors, yet there are a surprising number of ways to foul up.

Sure, it'll fit, and with a healthy squeeze on the crimping tool you may even get it trapped in there so it seems secure. The problem is that even if the large barrel on the terminal doesn't split from being over-crimped, it will not deform enough to completely surround the small-gauge wire, leaving only a small area of metal-to-metal contact, and a large amount of empty space that invites corrosion.

Then there is the issue of the quality of the goods. To save a few cents per thousand, some manufacturers of cheap and nasty solderless connectors, mostly from off-shore, will run multiple sizes of connector through the same stamping dies, only taking account of the varying barrel diameters at a later stage when the barrel itself is formed. As a result, the material in the area of the barrel in the larger size(s) may be thinned out excessively, leading to insecure crimps even when applied correctly. Though most solderless connectors have an open seam along the side of the barrel, top grade ones, as used in aircraft applications, have their seams brazed shut. As with everything else, you generally get what you pay for.

Finally, there is the matter of tools and technique. We discuss selection of a crimping tool in chapter eleven; here's how to perform the actual crimping. Just enough insulation should be stripped from the wire to leave a bared section of conductor just long enough to extend through the barrel of the connector. (Ironically, the improved tear resistance that characterizes better-quality insulation makes it significantly more difficult to strip; the cheap stuff is much easier to work with!) The connector barrel should be arranged in the jaws of the crimping tool so that the seam in the barrel lies in the concave recess in one jaw, while the dimple in the other jaw con-

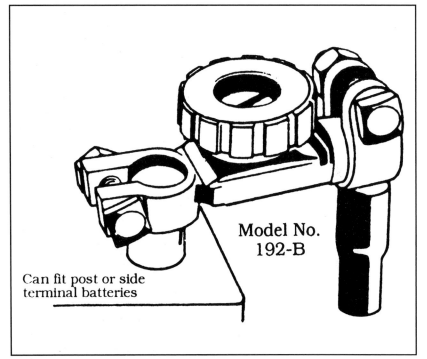

Can fit post or side terminal batteries

Model No. 192-B

A battery master switch is good insurance against serious grief if a short circuit should ever develop. To be useful, though, you have to be able to get at it. An in-line type, rather than this sort that mounts right at the battery terminal, is preferable. *Courtesy Antique Auto Battery Manufacturing Co.*

tacts the opposite side of the barrel. This applies even in the case of connectors with brazed barrels, though the seam may be much harder to see. Then, one firm squeeze, a tug on the wire to ensure it's tight, and you're done, though you can give a second crimp if you want.

If you do solder (and there are a few places where there is not much option), then you should know how to do it correctly. The first consideration is the solder itself, which should be either 60:40 or 63:37 type, with a resin core. The numbers denote the ratio of tin to lead; "resin core" means there are one or more thin strands of resin flux running down the center of the solder wire. The flux rapidly flows through the joint under the heat of the soldering operation, reacts with the film of oxide on the surfaces being joined, and floats it harmlessly away, so helping to ensure a sound electrical path. The brittle, shiny brown stuff visible at the edges of the finished joint is this mixture of flux and oxide.

Acid-core solder, used for plumbing repairs, must *never* be used in electrical work; the residue of the acid-based flux will promote corrosion later. Beware: The lettering that designates the type of solder eventually tends to rub off the label on the roll; the only sure way to avoid confusion and potential grief is to never allow acid-core solder into your electrical tool box.

We consider selection of the soldering iron itself in chapter eleven. Whatever choice you might make, the following points should be born in mind. Since copper is an excellent conductor of heat, as well as of electricity, we need to put heat into the joint much faster than the wire can carry it away, for a couple of reasons. First, if the joint cools too rapidly during the soldering process, you can be left with something called a "cold joint." If the solder is chilled too fast, it solidifies into a mass of crystals that is both mechanically weak and inferior as an electrical conductor. It is easy to spot this fault—the solder has a grainy, gray appearance quite unlike the smooth, shiny, silvery surface of a good soldered joint. (The 63:37 solder causes fewer problems of this kind and is used almost universally in the electronics industry.) Second, the soldering has to be carried out before the heat transmitted along the wire can melt or burn the insulation.

Soldering Technique

Soldering is not particularly difficult, but there are a few specific procedural notes. First, remem-

---

Acid-core solder, used for plumbing repairs, must never be used in electrical work; the residue of the acid-based flux will promote corrosion later.

---

ber that the solder is there to provide an electrical joint only; ensure that it will not be called on to provide a mechanical connection. This should not be a problem with crimped connectors, but can be elsewhere. Second, the surfaces to be soldered must be clean and free of oxidation; freshly stripped wire will be fine just as it is, but old lamp sockets, etc., may need to be attacked with a wire brush. If the surfaces of the working end of the soldering iron are not bright and shiny, you should file them lightly until they are. Next, heat up the iron and "tin" its tip by touching the end of the solder wire to the hot tip of the iron. The solder should flow uniformly over the surface, and this coating will help in transferring heat rapidly and uniformly to the joint.

Then, you heat the joint; the best approach is to lay the tip of the soldering iron in contact with the underside of the joint. Now, working from above, touch the solder to the joint—*not* to the tip of the iron. If the work is hot enough, the solder will instantly flow into the joint; if not, just wait a couple of seconds more. Once the solder has flowed, keep the heat on for a couple of seconds—as noted above, if the solder cools too fast, it will form a grainy cold joint. A cold joint may also occur if the joint is mechanically jarred while the solder is cooling, so hold everything steady for a slow five count after the heat is shut off. That's all there is to it! (Most people omit it, but if you want a real pro job, you should separately tin the surfaces that are to be joined before bringing them together.)

Whether soldered or not, the connection needs to be protected against corrosion (the plastic sleeve that comes on solderless connectors is there for electrical insulation only; it will not exclude moisture). This weather-proof seal can be achieved by wrapping tightly with electrical tape, by applying a brush-on or spray-on insulation, or with heat-shrink tubing. Though it is a bit more expensive, the best heat-shrink tubing is lined with a hot melt adhesive, to help ensure this tight seal.

A worthwhile supplementary step, once all the connections are made, is to smear a dielectric compound over the outside of every place where moisture may intrude; one such material is Dow Corning Compound 5. It can be applied to soldered connections, to mechanical joints where terminals are screwed or plugged together, and around the outside of the joints between high-tension leads and the distributor cap. When spread around the gap between bayonet type bulbs and their sockets, it also prevents them from seizing. On no account, however, use RTV silicone caulk—the stuff that smells like vinegar. That smell is acetic acid, which is released during curing of the rubber; the acid can later corrode the connection.

Checking and "Dressing" the Harness

Do-it-yourself restorers usually work neatly, electricians often don't. While a mechanic's wiring job may initially produce surprises such as wipers that sweep when you press on the brake or fuses that blow when you turn on the wipers, at least the wiring *looks* good! An electrician, on the other hand, is concerned first that everything works as advertised;

making the results look pretty is a secondary consideration. If you've stayed with us this far, by now you likely have an electrically-sound harness; to make a finished, professional job, you need to gather the individual wires together into neat bundles. But first, you should carefully check your work—it is much easier to correct problems at this stage than after the wires are bundled, or "loomed," and installed in the car. Check each circuit for continuity and ensure that the tags you have used at both ends of each conductor, to identify what goes where, make sense and agree with each other.

To group the collection of wires into a bundle, you can simply use nylon tie-wraps, installed at intervals of about 8 or 10 inches, with an extra one every place

one or more wires branch off from the main group. Alternatively, flexible-plastic sleeve material is available to gather the individual wires, or the whole package can be wrapped with overlapping turns of loom tape, or even ordinary electrical tape. Finally, recall that some of the specialty aftermarket harness makers will braid a fabric loom covering over your assembled harness.

Obviously, grommets should be used where wiring passes through holes in sheet metal, to protect against abrasion. Clips or clamps of some sort are also needed to hold the loom in place. If the original clips are missing or broken, they can be replaced with clamps of nylon or rubber-coated metal, secured by sheet metal screws or pop rivets.

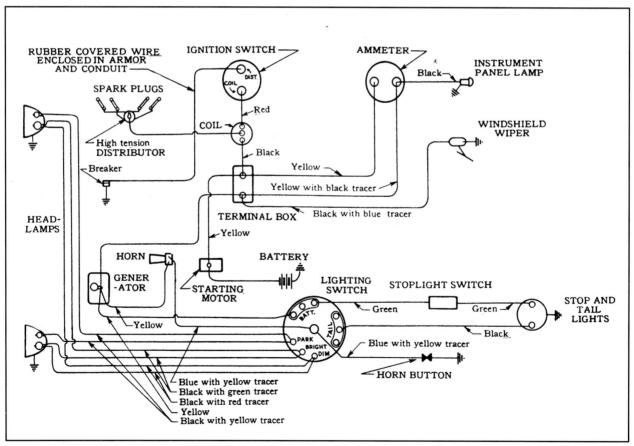

The electrical system on early cars—here a 1930 Model A is illustrated—was about as complex as the one on your Christmas tree. *Courtesy Ford Canada*

Fuses and Circuit Breakers

Even the most carefully executed electrical system can develop short circuits. Insulation can be worn through by sharp metal edges, motors and other components can develop internal shorts, and there is always the possibility of an accident that crushes body work, grounding a live conductor. When this happens, a dangerously large amount of current can flow, possibly damaging other, unaffected components such as switches, and creating lots of heat. At worst, a fire can result. To guard against this, fuses or circuit breakers are used to protect the circuit by breaking the electrical connection if ever the current should exceed safe limits. All automotive wiring, except for the starter circuit, should be protected in this way.

A fuse is just a carefully calibrated piece of wire that melts when the current passing through it exceeds some reference value. Though some very old vehicles

---

A worthwhile supplementary step, once all the connections are made, is to smear a dielectric compound over the outside of every place where moisture may intrude.

---

used a simple length of fuse wire to connect two terminals at a fuse block, by far the most common type is the familiar Buss fuse with a glass body and metal end caps that just snap into and out of a pair of miniature clips on the fuse block. They come in two different lengths and in a wide range of amperage ratings. Replaceable fuses like this have the advantage that there is no need to fiddle about stringing a new length of fuse wire when one "blows," and because less finger clearance is required, a larger number of fuses can be accommodated in a given amount of space. Any new circuit that might be added needs to be protected, too. Depending on the degree of authenticity required, and as an alternative to changing the fuse block, an inline fuse holder can be installed.

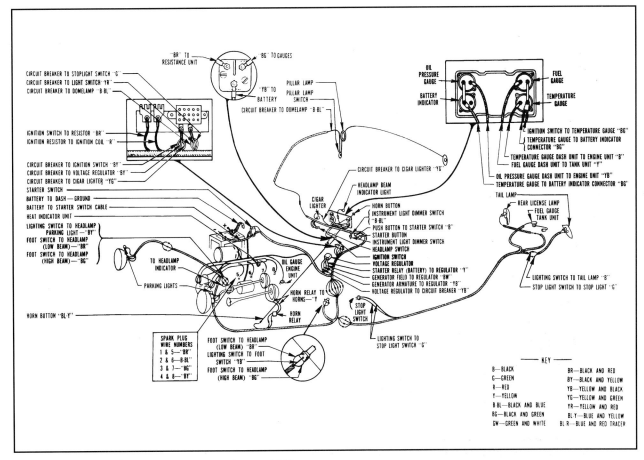

Electrical systems remained quite simple as late as 1940.

When a fuse blows, that's it—you're out of business until the fuse is replaced, and until the cause of the overload is found and corrected. To provide a sort of "limp-home" capability, some manufacturers have used circuit breakers instead of fuses. A circuit breaker uses the principle of the bimetallic strip that we have seen in IVRs, turn-signal flashers, and some dash gauges. When the current through the circuit breaker exceeds the designed limit, the heat causes a bimetallic strip to curve away from one of its contacts, breaking the circuit just as effectively as a conventional fuse. Unlike a fuse, though, the circuit breaker will re-connect the circuit after a short time, once it cools down. If the problem that caused the excessive current remains, the circuit breaker will cycle off and on indefinitely (though note that some modern cars have circuit breakers that stay blown until you push on a little external button to reset them).

If it comes to choosing between fuses and circuit breakers, there are arguments on both sides. On the one hand, there are situations where you would much rather have a component that works intermittently, even though there may be a problem in the circuit that feeds it, until you can get to safety and fix the problem. Wipers are a good example. On the other hand, a short in a circuit-breaker-protected circuit that is live even when the key is off will run the battery completely flat. That is inconvenient enough, but there is a worse case. If the odds are really stacked against you, a circuit breaker may allow enough juice through a damaged circuit during the times it is on that the heat gradually builds to the point that something catches fire. The writer came very close to having this happen on a 1960s Studebaker. Damaged dome-light wiring, cycling between off and dead short as the circuit breaker clicked off and on, grew

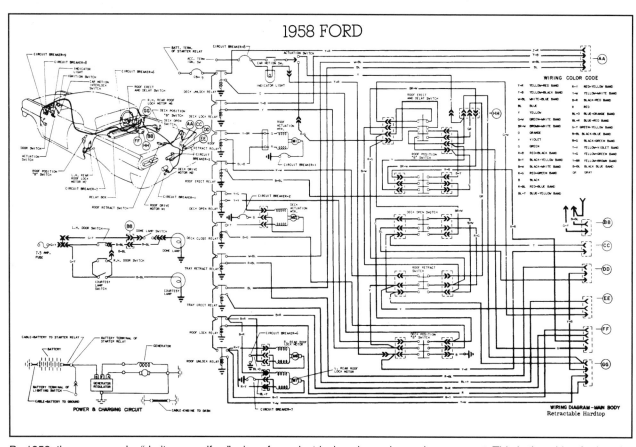

By 1958, the reasons why "do-it-yourselfers" cringe from electrical work was becoming apparent. This is the wiring for just the convertible top on a 1958 Ford. *Courtesy Ford Canada*

hot enough to scorch the roof liner. Fortunately, as it turned out, the battery ran flat before the car melted down. This kind of situation is rare, but it's possible, especially if the car is left unattended.

Here's how to select a fuse or circuit breaker for a new circuit, or an old one with upgraded wiring to cope with an increased load, say from beefier headlights.

First, establish the current draw of the circuit. (If the component has a fixed resistance, like lights, you can calculate the amperage from resistance and voltage measurements, using Ohm's Law; for components whose resistance varies, such as motors, you have to either measure the current draw directly with an ammeter or else use the technique suggested in the sidebar Indirectly Measuring Large Currents with a Multi-Meter in chapter eleven.) The correct fuse or circuit breaker should have an amperage rating that is just a little higher (say 15–20 percent) than the measured or calculated circuit current. If the rating is too close to the actual circuit draw, the fuse or circuit breaker will pop frequently; if far higher, there will be no effective protection.

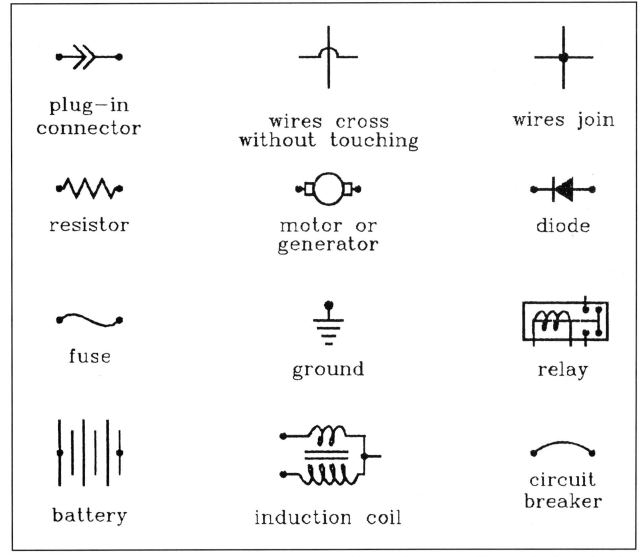

plug–in connector

wires cross without touching

wires join

resistor

motor or generator

diode

fuse

ground

relay

battery

induction coil

circuit breaker

The symbols used on wiring diagrams are often simplified drawings of the parts they represent. Here are a few that are less than obvious. *Courtesy Ford Canada*

Tools

11

We assume that anyone involved in other aspects of automotive repair or restoration work will already have the usual collection of wrenches, sockets, screwdrivers, and so on needed for dismantling and assembling mechanical parts. These, of course, will see frequent use when working on electrical equipment. Beyond that, the tools required specifically for electrical work on vehicles of the pre-electronics era are few in number and inexpensive, so there is little excuse for skimping on their quality.

Testing Continuity

For tracing electrical paths and identifying open or short circuits, the choice lies between a simple "continuity tester" and a volt-ohmmeter. At its simplest, a continuity tester is simply a light bulb and socket with a length of wire connected to each terminal of the bulb; when power runs through the tester, the bulb lights up, powered by the circuit being tested. To free up your hands, an alligator clip can be fitted to the end of either or both wires. In some cases, it may be advisable to splice an inline fuse holder (with fuse) into one of the test-probe leads; that way, if a dead short is encountered the fuse will blow, rather than the current melting a defective circuit, or the tester.

While making such a simple tool requires no more talent or time than making toast, there is a commercially available variant worth considering. It looks a bit like an ice-pick with a single wire protruding out of the end of its handle. The circuit within the tester runs from its sharp tip,

through a light bulb protected within the transparent plastic handle, to an alligator clip on the end of the wire. To check the continuity of a circuit, the alligator clip is typically fastened to a ground—such as a point on the metal chassis of the vehicle, scraped to bare metal free of paint, dirt, and rust—and the point of the tester is touched to a terminal that is supposed to be hot. If it is, the bulb will light.

The sharp point is convenient for working in confined areas—checking each contact in a

---

For straightforward troubleshooting, a simple continuity tester as described should be regarded as essential equipment.

---

multi-pin connector, for example—and allows the probe to be pushed through the insulation on wires to permit identifying just which wire in a bundle is the live one. (When you're done, the puncture caused by the spike should be sealed over, either with a tight wrap of electrical tape or with one of the brush-on "liquid-tape" formulations.) Such externally powered testers are dirt cheap, extremely useful for troubleshooting, and convenient—they will stow in a pocket, though there is a risk of spearing yourself in the hip! Just be sure to get the kind

intended for low-voltage automotive work. (A similar device intended for use on 110-volt household circuits simply won't work on 12- or 6-volt systems, though there are others that work at any voltage, either AC or DC.)

For straightforward troubleshooting, a simple continuity tester as described should be regarded as essential equipment. It has the drawback, however, that it gives only a "yes" or no" readout; it can tell you whether or not there is a complete circuit, but except for sometimes faint variations in the brightness of the bulb, it can't tell you anything about the current or voltage on that circuit, or its resistance. More information is often needed.

Using a continuity tester, for example, you might establish that the circuit to a brake-light bulb is working correctly—the test lamp lights up when the brake pedal is pressed. But, unless a bulb has blown, you already knew that—the brake light comes on! What you may want to know is why the brake light burns so dimly. You suspect that it is a funky ground, but is the bad connection between the bulb and the socket? Between the socket and the brake-light housing? Between the housing and the fender? The fender and the chassis? A continuity tester can't tell you that.

Multi-Meters

To determine the actual voltage or resistance between two points, you need a voltmeter or ohmmeter. These two functions are combined in one unit called a multi-meter or volt-ohmmeter. An ammeter function is also usually included, but beware: Most multimeters are designed for use in electronics work, where currents are measured in *milliamps*—thousandths of an amp; while these inexpensive units are fine for making voltage and resistance measurements, they usually cannot handle the currents found in many automotive circuits when used as an ammeter.

Most of the cost of these contraptions is in the meter itself, rather than any of the internal components, so while a serviceable instrument can be had for as little as $10, for just a little more money you can get one with a meter face that is much larger, and therefore more readable. We're speaking here of an *analog*-type meter—the kind with a dial face and moving needle; there is also the option of a *digital* multimeter, which simply shows a number on its face. The difference in the read-out is just like that between a digital wristwatch and the conventional kind.

Apart from the nature of the display, which is mostly a matter of personal preference (though there is an advantage to an instrument that can be clearly read in the dark), most of the advantages of digital meters apply to electronics work; they are of little benefit in the kind of automotive work we are discussing here.

To explain, although an analog multi-meter is designed so that it has a very high internal resistance, it is still not a perfect insulator. In other words, it consumes a minuscule but measurable amount of power just in the act of moving the needle. When you use one to measure the voltage drop across a component, for example, you are in fact connecting a second, parallel circuit around the component being tested. Because the current draw of automotive equipment is comparatively large—in other words, the resistance of the component is

Indirectly Measuring Large Currents with a Multi-Meter

As mentioned, most inexpensive, general-purpose multi-meters include a few amps scales; unfortunately, the highest available amperage scale usually lies well below what is needed to measure the comparatively large currents found in automotive circuits. As an alternative to shelling out for a premium-priced unit, we have suggested the possibility of using a regular automobile ammeter for this purpose. A drawback to this is the relative insensitivity of such an instrument. Using an ammeter with a 2-inch face and a maximum reading of 30 amps, for example, it will be difficult to read a 2- or 3-amp draw with any degree of accuracy—the width of the needle may span a couple of amps.

It is, however, possible to use a multi-meter for indirectly measuring currents far in excess of the basic capacity of the ammeter function of the instrument. For example, suppose we want to measure the current draw of a 12-volt wiper motor. In principle, it seems we could measure the resistance of the motor, and the voltage drop across it, and then use Ohm's Law to figure the current based on those other two values. Trouble is, the motor's resistance depends on how hard it is working, and we cannot measure the resistance of the motor while power is being fed to it.

The trick is to insert some small known resistance into the motor circuit, and measure the voltage drop across that resistor. Then we can make use of Ohm's Law to calculate the current through the resistor. Because the two are connected in series, this must be the same as the current through the motor. We can guess that the current will be some small number of amps—maybe 2 or 3. (Note that the highest scale on the multi-meter, however, may only read to 250 milliamps—one quarter of an amp. As little as 1/2 an amp through the meter might hurt it; 4 or 5 would fry it for sure.)

As a starting place for our calculations, let's assume the motor draws 2 amps. Approximately, then, the resistance represented by the running motor would be calculated as follows:

$$\frac{12 \text{ volts}}{2 \text{ amps}} = 6 \text{ ohms}$$

We have to perform this rough calculation first because we need to select a resistance that is some small fraction of that of the motor. Let's use 0.6 ohms—one tenth that of our "guesstimate." We also have to ensure the resistor will dissipate the heat it develops. Since we're guessing that the motor draws 2 amps at 12 volts, then the motor's power consumption is calculated as follows:

$$2 \text{ amps} \times 12 \text{ volts} = 24 \text{ watts}$$

With roughly one tenth the resistance, the resistor will account for about 2-1/2 watts; better get a 5-watt unit, just to be on the safe side.

Now, wire the resistor in series with the motor, turn on the power, and confirm the supply voltage by measuring across the battery terminals with the motor running under the representative load of wiping a wet windshield. (Don't just assume this is 12 volts, or 6. First, battery-terminal voltage is seldom exactly at the nominal figure; second, the load of the motor will pull the battery voltage down a little.) Let's say you read 11.0 volts. Next, measure the voltage drop across the resistor while the motor is running. Let's say that figure is 1.5 volts. From Ohm's Law, the current through the resistor can be calculated:

$$\frac{1.5 \text{ volts}}{0.6 \text{ ohms}} = 2.5 \text{ amps}$$

Because the current is constant through this series circuit, this calculated current must be the same as the current through the motor. *Voila*!

A bench-type multi-meter is beyond the needs and budget of the average restorer. Still, it's about the only way to directly measure large currents.

comparatively low—very little current flows through the additional high-resistance path of the test meter, so the effect on the voltage reading is negligible.

By contrast, the currents in electronic gear (radios, TVs, computers, etc.) are extremely tiny, so it is vitally important to avoid affecting the thing being measured with the instrument doing the measuring. A digital multi-meter has an internal resistance

many times greater than that of the analog type, and so digital multi-meters are the only multi-meters that read accurately on sensitive electronic circuits. That is not to suggest that a digital meter is not suitable for automotive electrical work; if you have one, by all means use it.

There are only two drawbacks to a digital multi-meter, from our point of view. First, they are considerably more expensive;

second, their internal circuitry requires a small amount of time to respond to a change in the factor being measured. As a result of that last, they not only have a tendency to "hunt" (flicker endlessly between 12.01 volts and 12.02, for example) even when what is being applied is, for our purposes, a constant value, they also may either fail to respond at all to a brief change in the signal or else give a crazy, constantly

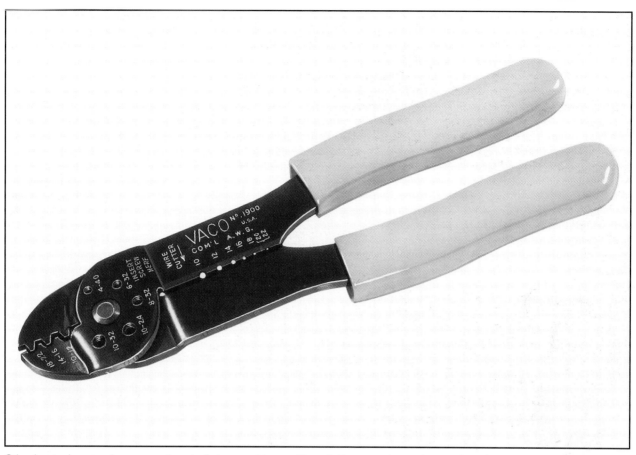

Crimping tools come in an assortment of sizes and types. Though there are general purpose tools, ones specialized for either insulated or non-insulted terminals, do a better job at their specialty than the generic type. *Courtesy Klein Tools*

changing flutter of numbers that is impossible to read. An analog meter is better at showing the kind of momentary variations that can occur when, for example, you wiggle a wire with an internal fracture. The needle on the analog meter will flick each time the circuit makes or breaks; under the same circumstances, a digital unit might never settle down to a readable number at all, or blithely continue to flick between 12.01 and 12.02 volts!

In addition to providing a quantitative reading ("how much," not simply "yes" or "no"), the resistance measuring function of a multi-meter has the benefit that it can be used when the circuit is not live; a small battery within the meter makes it self-powered. While this is a considerable advantage when working

> The needle on the analog meter will flick each time the circuit makes or breaks; under the same circumstances, a digital unit might never settle down to a readable number at all, or blithely continue to flick between 12.01 and 12.02 volts!

on wiring or components off the car, it can also be a source of grief: If any attempt is made to measure the resistance of a live circuit, not only will a false reading result, it is also likely that the meter will be irreparably damaged. On the other hand, the voltage function obviously only returns useful information when the circuit is powered.

Because of the wide variety of applications in which these instruments are used, a multi-meter is equipped with a selector knob that allows adjusting the sensitivity of the meter according to the magnitude of the variable being measured; the meter face itself has separate scales, each corresponding to one setting of the selector switch. For instance, on the general purpose multi-meter this writer bought for about $20 an equal number of years ago there is a selection among full-scale readings of 0.25,

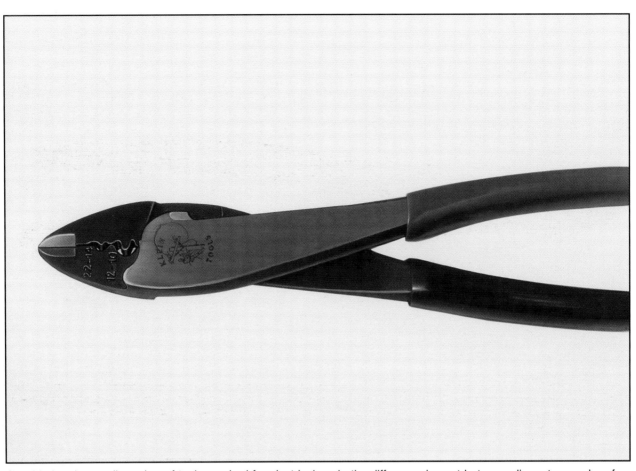

Considering the small number of tools required for electrical work, the difference in cost between dime-store and professional quality tools is insignificant. *Courtesy Klein Tools*

10, 50, 250, 500, and 1,000 volts DC; among 1, 100, and 1,000 ohms; and among 0.5, 25, and 250 milliamps. For most automotive work, the 10- or 50-volt scale would be used; resistance measurements might be on any of the three scales.

For the size of currents drawn by even the smallest loads encountered in vehicle electrics, the ammeter section of this and similar inexpensive general purpose multi-meters is next to useless. For the sort of work we're dealing with here, you want to be able to measure currents up to at least 10 amps; 30 would be better. Similar meters are available with a greatly expanded range of amperage scales, but ones with a capacity of even 10 amps are significantly more expensive, so it may prove more advantageous to

acquire a separate, single-purpose ammeter for current readings. (But see also the sidebar Indirectly Measuring Large Currents with a Multi-Meter.)

Using a Multi-Meter

When using a meter to establish what's going on in an automotive electrical circuit, there are four essential points to remember:

1. The voltage drop across a component is measured across the two terminals of the component (bearing in mind, of course, that one of the terminals may be the case or housing that connects the component to ground), so the meter is connected *in parallel* with the component.

2. The resistance within a component is likewise measured *in parallel* with the component.

3. Resistance should only ever be measured on an un-powered circuit; *never* connect an ohmmeter (including a multi-meter switched to an ohms scale) to a live circuit—you'll fry the meter.

4. The current through a component is measured by placing the meter *in series* with the component; all the juice has to pass through the meter, which is why you can't use an inexpensive general purpose multi-meter to measure, say, the output of a generator or the current draw of a wiper motor.

Multi-meters are always supplied with a pair of lead wires, usually with a fitting on each end—a short one that plugs into the meter, and a longer probe for poking at the circuit. Replace-

120

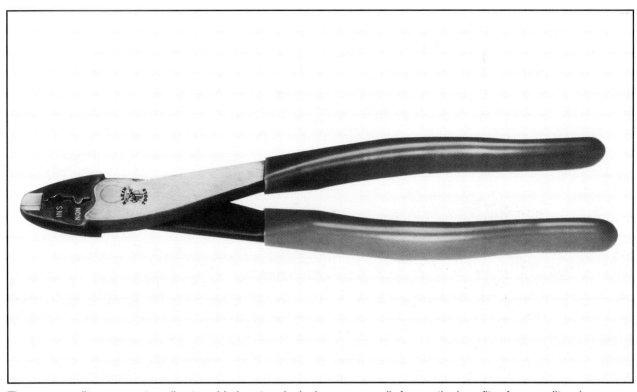

The same quality argument applies to solderless terminal crimpers, as well. Among the benefits of pro-quality crimpers are sturdier construction and plastic hand grips that reduce wear and tear on your hands. *Courtesy Klein Tools*

ment leads with a matching short pin probe on one end and an alligator clip on the other are readily available at electronics- and tool-supply stores; these offer the convenience, in many situations, of freeing up one hand. It is also possible to separately buy the end fittings—probes and alligator clips—and to solder up your own leads. The assembled leads are so inexpensive, though, that it is usually not worth the bother, unless you need some soldering practice.

While you're buying or making test leads, you will also want an assortment of jumper leads—simply lengths of wire with clips on both ends to allow "skipping" around components or supplying juice to a component off the car. For versatility, the wire itself should be of a sufficiently hefty gauge to safely carry the largest current likely to be encountered; #10 gauge should be adequate for both 6- and 12-volt

> For less than the price of a six-pack of beer you can get a tool that combines wire cutters, a variety of precisely proportioned semi-circular openings for insulation stripping, and specially shaped jaws for crimping solderless connectors of various sizes.

systems—except, of course, for feeding the starter!

While ammeters are made that can cope with hundreds or even thousands of amps, these industrial-strength units are physically large and seriously

expensive. The only practical way of measuring the current draw of an automobile starter is with an inductive ammeter. This is a device with a conventional gauge face, but no apparent way to hook it up. On the back, though, is something that looks like a broom clip; this U-shaped bracket is simply slipped over the outside of the insulated cable carrying the current. The instrument actually measures the strength of the electromagnetic field around the conductor and displays the result directly in amps.

Tools for Wiring

There are some other items to add to your electrical tool kit. For less than the price of a six-pack of beer you can get a tool that combines wire cutters, a variety of precisely proportioned semi-circular openings for insulation stripping, and specially shaped jaws for crimping solderless connectors of various sizes. Note

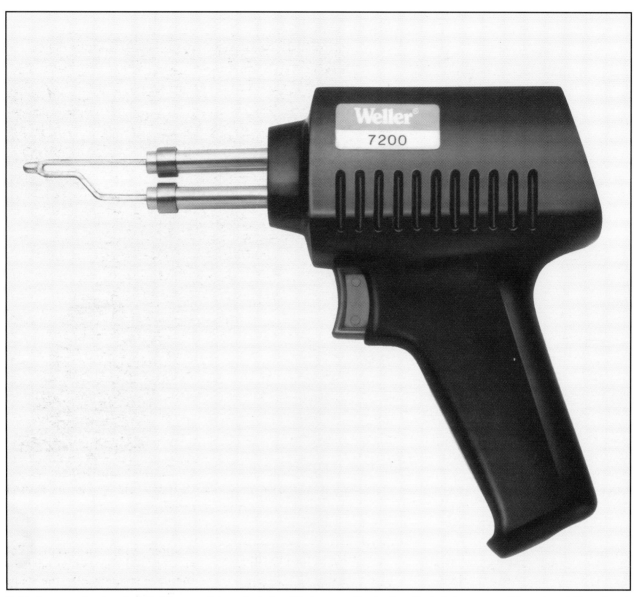

Soldering guns heat up fast, but they cool down fast also. That means they're less likely to burn something when left unattended, but it also increases the risk of a "cold" joint. This is a single-range model. *Courtesy Cooper Tools*

that the design of the crimping jaws sometimes depends on whether the connectors to be used are insulated or not—choose the type designed for the type of connector you intend to use. The more expensive of these tools have sturdier construction and cushioned rubber handles to reduce the wear and tear on your hands. Sadly, even the better brands tend to be better at the stripping and crimping functions than at doing a clean job of cut-

ting multi-strand wire—one or two strands always seem to require an extra couple of nibbles. In addition, then, you should have a good sharp pair of side cutters. On no account, though, should you use a blade of any sort for the wire stripping; it is just too easy to nick the fine strands of conductor. Likewise, while it is possible to do the crimping with pliers, a purpose-designed tool will reduce waste and make the task a lot easier.

We discussed the pros and cons of soldering versus crimped, solderless connectors in the previous chapter. Whichever side of this argument you may come down on, you are bound to encounter situations where there is no alternative to soldering. That brings us to the matter of choosing a soldering iron.

Soldering Irons

For most automotive wiring applications the choice is

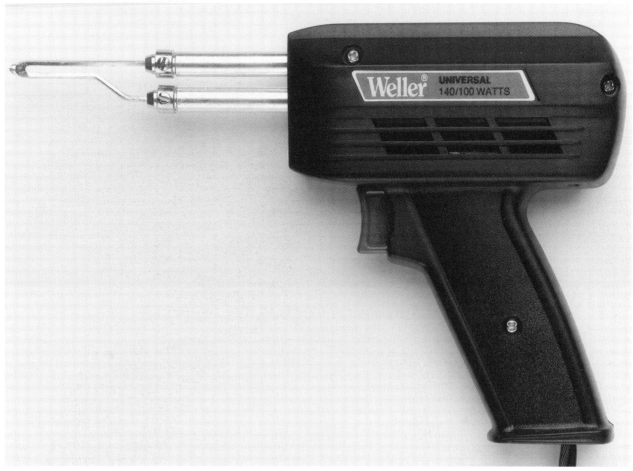

Soldering guns heat up fast, but they cool down fast also. That means they're less likely to burn something when left unattended, but it also increases the risk of a "cold" joint. This is a dual-range models. *Courtesy Cooper Tools*

between the gun-type and the smaller, pencil-type irons. The gun-type irons put out somewhere between, say, 100 and 300 watts, depending on the model (there are also dual-heat-range models that are switchable between a high and a low setting). The pencil-type tools are typically of 20 to 40 watts, though there are also models up to 100 watts or more. The pistol-grip, instant-on irons have the advantage of a very rapid warm-up and cool-down, so they can safely be set down to free up your hands without much risk of melting or burning anything, and properly handled, they can offer the kind of big, brief slug of heat needed to get the joint up to temperature without overheating

> For automotive wiring, either a lower-powered gun-type or a pencil-type in the higher wattage ranges can produce satisfactory results, and the choice probably boils down to personal preference.

adjacent insulation. By the same token, "instant-on" also means "instant-off," so if the trigger switch is released too early, the cold-joint problem discussed in

chapter ten can occur. You should hold the switch on for a couple of seconds after the solder begins to flow.

For automotive wiring, either a lower-powered gun-type or a pencil-type in the higher wattage ranges can produce satisfactory results, and the choice probably boils down to personal preference. The drawback to the pencil type is the need for some sort of rest on which to set down the hot iron, to avoid the risk of burns and fire. Conversely, though not likely a problem for vehicles of the era we are dealing with in this book, it is worth noting that the various electronic black boxes in more modern cars contain delicate integrated circuits that can be damaged by the

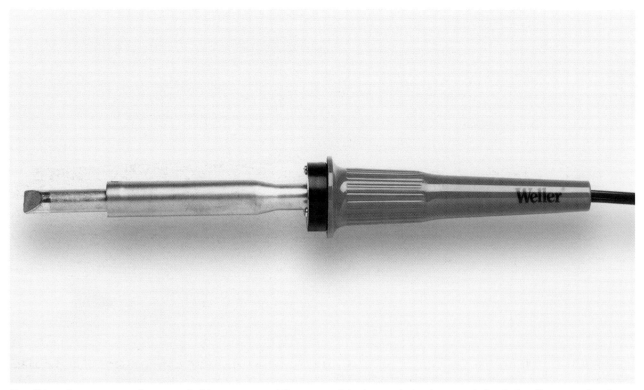

Pencil-type irons are usually somewhat lower-powered than guns, take longer to heat up, and stay hot until you unplug them. *Courtesy Cooper Tools*

strong magnetic field produced by the transformer in gun-type irons.

Other Soldering Tools

Apart from the solder itself (see chapter ten), there are a few additional items that, while not absolutely necessary, make soldering easier and cost next to nothing. All are available at the same place you would buy a soldering iron. One is a double-ended tool with a simple pick at one end and a twin-pronged fitting at the other, like a small fork. This will prove invaluable when *unsoldering* connections; the fork end gets a good grip on the wire and allows it to be levered out of the way once the solder has been melted by the application of heat from the soldering gun. A nifty little device is also available to clean up the excess of solder that accumulates around a joint that has been disconnected in this way. This consists of a squeeze bulb made of heat-resistant rubber that is fitted with a small nozzle made from Teflon or another strongly heat-resistant plastic. In use, the solder is melted by the iron, then the bulb is squeezed to suction up the molten solder. Finally, a damp sponge (and something to set it on) will prove very handy for wiping excess solder and flux off the end of a hot iron.

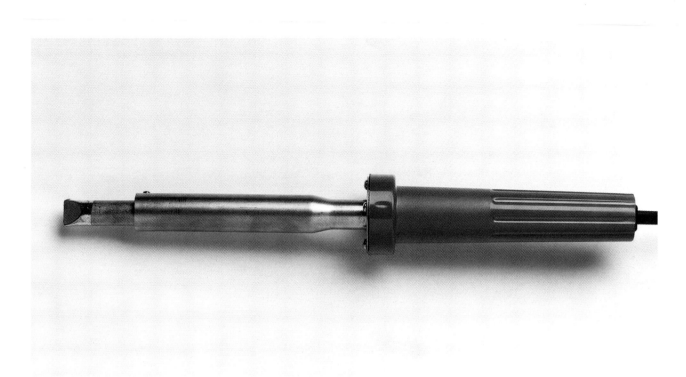

The steady heat of pencil-type irons is a plus for working on fine wiring, but can be a hazard if you're not careful. The slim profile helps when working in tight quarters. *Courtesy Cooper Tools*

Tables

Minimum Gauge of Wire Versus Length of Run (12-Volt Systems)

Current (amps)	Length (feet)					
	5	10	15	20	25	30
5				18	18	18
7			18	18	16	16
10		18	16	16	16	16
12		18	16	16	14	14
15		18	14	14	12	12
18	18	16	14	14	12	12
20	18	16	14	12	10	10
24	18	16	12	10	10	10
30	16	14	10	10	10	10
40	16	12	10	10	8	8
50	14	12	10	10	8	8

Minimum Gauge of Wire Versus Length of Run (6-Volt Systems)

Current (amps)	Length (feet)					
	5	10	15	20	25	30
5				16	16	16
7			16	16	14	14
10		16	14	14	14	14
12		16	14	14	12	12
15		16	12	12	10	10
18	16	14	12	12	10	10
20	16	14	12	10	8	8
24	16	14	10	8	8	8
30	14	12	8	8	8	8
40	14	10	8	8	6	6
50	12	10	8	8	6	6

Amps to Reach Temperature Limit of Insulation

Insulation Type:

	Polyethylene; Neoprene; Polyurethane; semi-rigid PVC	Polypropylene High-density polyethylene	irradiated PVC; Nylon	cross-linked Polyethylene; thermoplastic elastomers	Kapton Silicon Teflon
Copper temp.	176°	194°	221°	257°	392°
Gauge					
#20	10	12	13	14	17
#18	15	17	18	20	24
#16	19	22	24	26	32
#14	27	30	33	40	45
#12	36	40	45	50	55
#10	47	55	58	70	75

Parts Sources

A&S Products, Inc.
6270 Sterling Dr.
Newport, MI 48166
(reproduction ignition coils)

American Plastic Chrome
1398 Mar Ann
Westland, MI 48185
(re-plating plastic)

Antique Auto Battery
Manufacturing Co.
2320 Old Mill Rd.
Hudson, OH 44236
(dual-voltage batteries and Orpin
series/parallel switches)

Antique Auto Electric
58 Blake St. E.
Goderich, ON
CANADA N7A 1C8
(starter and generator repair and
rewinding, ignition parts)

Aromat
919 Kamato Rd.
Mississauga, ON
CANADA L4W 2R5
(6-volt relays)

Donald I. Axelrod
35 Timson St.
Lynn, MA 01902
(headlights, lenses, etc.)

Bathurst, Inc.
P.O. Box 27
Tyrone, PA 16686
(batteries and master switches)

Becker Sales
R.R. 519 Wyoming Ave.
West Pittston, PA 18643
(electrical equipment for collector
cars)

Dennis Carpenter Reproductions
P.O. Box 26398
Charlotte, NC 28221-6398
(ignition coil for Ford flatheads)

Fifth Avenue Auto Parts
502 Arthur Ave.
Clay Center, KS 67432
(6-volt alternators)

Bob Groulx
1970 Buena Vista
Livermore, CA 94550
(starter and generator repair, battery
cables)

Harnesses Unlimited
P.O. Box 435
Wayne, PA 19087
(wiring harnesses and braiding
service)

M&H Electric Fabricators, Inc.
13537 Alondra Blvd.
Santa Fe Springs, CA 90670
(wiring harnesses)

Mr. G's
5613 Elliott Reeder Rd.
Fort Worth, TX 76117
(re-plated plastic side and tail-lamp
reflectors)

Narragansett Reproductions
P.O. Box 51
Wood River Junction, RI 02894
(wiring harnesses and molded
connectors)

New Castle Battery Mfg. Co.
P.O. Box 5040
New Castle, PA 16105
(reproduction batteries)

Optima Batteries, Inc.
9 E. Mississippi Ave.
Denver, CO 80210
(batteries)

M. Parker Autoworks, Inc.
374 N. Cooper Rd., Unit C-7
Berlin, NJ 08009
(wiring harnesses for 1955–1975 GM
products)

PMX Custom Alternators
2029 SE 9th
Portland, OR 97214
(6- and 12-volt alternators)

Rhode Island Wiring Service, Inc.
P.O. Box 434 H
West Kingston, RI 02892
(wiring harnesses)

Uvira
310 Pleasant Valley Rd.
Merlin, OR 97532
(headlight-reflector renovation)

YnZ's Yesterday's Parts
333 E. Stuart Ave.
Redlands, CA 92374
(wiring harnesses)

Index